INDIE GAMING

INDIE GAMING

FINDING ENTREPRENEURIAL
SUCCESS IN VIDEO GAMES

BRIAN BIES

NEW DEGREE PRESS

INDIE GAMING

Finding Entrepreneurial Success in Video Games

ISBN   978-1-5445-0006-5 *Paperback*

         978-1-5445-0007-2 *Ebook*

Dedicated to my parents, sister, and Riley for all of their love and support. This book is for Ralph H. Baer, who dared to innovate and challenge the status quo.

CONTENTS

"In the modern world of business, it is useless to be a creative, original thinker unless you can also sell what you create."

— DAVID OGILVY, CO-FOUNDER OF OGILVY & MATHER

INTRODUCTION

———

"The only way to get an education is read, read, read, read, read anything. That's how I learned English, that's how I learned poetry."

— RALPH BAER ("THE FATHER OF VIDEO GAMES")

November 2012. I was in Manchester, New Hampshire. I was there to interview Ralph Baer for my high school's Oral History Project. Ralph Baer is most commonly known as the "**Father of Video Games**," inventor of the first video game console.

My hands were shaking – I was sweating. I was wearing a tie in my attempt to look professional, but it was clear that I was nervous. After all, I was interviewing an influential person in history. Moreover, he was someone who played a pivotal role in my life. If not for Ralph Baer's ingenuity, which inspired him to make the Magnavox Odyssey, the *first* video game console, and the basis for the founding of the video game industry, I would not be able to call myself a gamer.

But the funny story is when I showed up to his house, he was outside putting some trash out by the curb and he asked me who I was. I blurted, "Hi, I'm Brian. I'm a Junior at St. Andrew's Episcopal School in Potomac, MD. We have talked about and agreed that I would interview you on this date and time." After a short moment, he responded to me, "Oh, Okay. Come inside."

We entered his house, and he took me to his office — that was to be the place where we conducted the interview — and we sat down.

As I was setting up the recording equipment up, he started asking me about why I wanted to interview him. It was as if he was testing me to see if he should give me his time to interview him. It might seem funny now, but in the moment it was beyond terrifying. I honestly had no idea that his reaction was going to be and whether or not I had flown up to Manchester, New Hampshire for nothing.

I explained, "I am here to interview you because in the junior year of high school, every student must complete a project known as the "Oral History Project," where we interview someone who was present at a particular event or time in history." The vast majority of people interview a Civil Rights Activist or a War Veteran. But I chose a different path. I wanted to interview someone who was in a field that I was passionate about.

Taking a step back, I had chosen Ralph Baer because he is "The Father of Video Games," the inventor of the *first* video game console. In other words, he was not simply present to witness a time or event in history: he *made* history.

As far as people to interview on "The Video Game Industry" and its founding, Ralph Baer would be the #1 person on the list. But interviewing someone on a topic, such as the video game industry, was outside the norm of what people did for the Oral History Project.

I am thankful that after grilling me that he agreed to the interview, because if he hadn't, I would have been up a creek without a paddle!

In the process of interviewing him, I had the opportunity to spend time up close and personal with a true entrepreneur, a true innovator in the fields of Science and Technology.

You see, it turns out that he was not just a video game inventor, but he had also accumulated:

- Over 150 U.S. and foreign patents
- Most notably, he invented The Magnavox Odyssey, the first video game console that was publicly sold (released in 1972)
- He had received extensive recognition for his contributions and impact, including receiving the National Medal of Technology in 2006 and induction in the National Inventors Hall of Fame in 2010.

So, I really was in awe of the fact that I got to interview him.

During the interview, he showed me around his house, I had lunch with him — he even showed me his lab. We ended up spending most of the day together. Ultimately, I had to leave to later in the afternoon, to make my flight back to Washington, DC. But the day was phenomenal for me. I got to speak with and interview a personal hero of mine and summarize it all in a 100+ page Oral History Project that documented his life, the advancements and technological changes that resulted from his work, and talk about the beginnings and the rise of the video game industry.

The **greatest highlight of my day** with him though was that not that I got this great opportunity to personally interact with him and learn his story—and that was *amazing*—but that I got to play him in Pong, the first sports arcade video game on his original Magnavox Odyssey Console.

He annihilated me (it should come as no surprise since it was his invention). I had originally wanted to play "The Best of 3." Quickly that became "the best of 5," then 7, and 9, and finally I gave up. *At the time, he was almost 91 and I was almost 16.*

By the age difference alone, any "rational" person might think that I would, under any set of normal circumstances, win by a mile. But, in fact, it was just the opposite: he decimated any attempt I made to win without even breaking a sweat.

I was embarrassed, the only solace I can take is that I played Ralph Baer, "The Father of Video Games" in Pong — which is an experience that not many people can say they have had.

Jumping forward to February 2013, I sent Ralph another email saying:

> "Interviewing you was such an impactful experience for me, you taught me so much. Could you point me in the direction of interviewing other people in the video game industry?"

My hope was that I could leverage this relationship that I had developed with Ralph to interview other people in the video game industry and create a blog about it. My goal was to interview innovators and pioneers — **entrepreneurs** — and recount their stories and learnings in a blog format that would bolster my understanding of the video game industry and gaming more generally.

Thirty minutes later he responded to my email and he copied a good friend of his to connect me with the pioneers and innovators in the video game industry.

For being 91 years old, he certainly was tech savvy. After one look at Ralph Baer, you might not expect much from him, but once you knew who he was, his response rate, his striking creative abilities and technological understanding makes sense on a much deeper level.

His friend forwarded a list of over 100 people for me to reach out to and possibly interview— all who were influential in the video game industry. Some of the people included:

- Richard Garriott, who pioneered the MMO genre with *Ultima*
- Gordon Walter, a lifetime entrepreneur in video game industry
- Burnie Burns, co-founder of Rooster Teeth and known for his contributions in *machinima*, a form of film making that uses video game technology in its production

They were all incredibly accomplished and talented people in the video game industry. I had their email addresses and the blessing to connect with them all within the span of a few hours.

By simply asking Ralph, I was given the keys to the "Kingdom" of the video game industry and built up a portfolio of work that showcased what I had learned and the network that I had developed.

I was Mario entering Princess Peach's Castle, but instead of getting a message saying, "Thank You Mario! But our Princess is in another castle!" I successfully found Princess Peach.

Over the summer following my junior year, I interviewed a number of different figures in the video game industry. I learned a lot about their experiences and stories as they relate to the video game industry as well as the video gaming culture. Specifically, I learned about how difficult it can be to join a team and work on a new project, how companies are cautious in "green lighting" a new IP, the challenges of working in obscurity, as well as the ultimate vindication of work well-received.

As a result of these conversations, I developed a perspective that I previously lacked when talking about the video game industry. When people talk about *Call of Duty* or the latest *Halo* or "insert practically any video game here," I have a different outlook on the culture of the video game industry, of what it means to talk about innovations and talk about the entrepreneurial process in the industry.

I now see video game companies through the **lens of business**, specifically as *established* companies, who are striving to be *entrepreneurial*, and the start-ups, who are focused on entrepreneurship and who are going through the process of starting a new company. By their very nature, I see Independent Game Developers to be **world-class entrepreneurs**.

My new perspective helped me see that, like entrepreneurs, those in the video game industry are doing more than making entertainment. They're making something from nothing, like starting a company from scratch. When you look at the video game industry and gaming at large, talking about these subjects with this lens in addition to everything else, something gets uncovered — it is a **story of empowerment**.

At the very core of the matter, Ralph Baer founded the video game industry and was an inventor who was also an entre-preneur. Because "The Father of Video Games" was an entrepreneur, in the very DNA of the video game industry exists the values of entrepreneurship as well. This is important because when talking about the video game industry in this way, it adds an incredible amount of value to the amazing work of a large number of people in the video game industry.

So, if the video game industry is a breeding ground for entre-preneurship, who are the best entrepreneurs in the space?

The answer: Independent Game Developers—or "Indie Developers." Independent Game Developers *are* entrepreneurs!

In taking this view it will allow Independent Game Developers to redefine the video game industry in how the industry is perceived by the media and the outside world as well as how Independent Game Developers view themselves and their work. This will allow Independent Game Developers to be more fully appreciated for their role and contributions to the video game industry.

The paradigm shift might seem subtle to an attuned gamer who understands very intuitively that Independent Game Developers are entrepreneurs, but the paradigm shift in a greater context will allow the Indie Developers to take their ideas and innovations to new heights and take over the video game space in a big way.

Independent Game Developers are what this book is all about — their stories, their lessons learned, and how they are the entrepreneurs of the video game industry today. Recognizing this fact will redefine what it means to be an entrepreneur in the video game industry, it will quite literally *change the game.* As the EA Sports slogan goes, "It's in the game." That "it" in this case is <u>entrepreneurship</u>.

My book is not about demonizing AAA Developers (e.g.,

Infinity Ward, Naughty Dog, Blizzard, BioWare, etc.) or major publishing companies such as EA, Ubisoft, and Activision. To be quite honest, I love all types of video games, and I have had my fair share of positive experiences playing *Call of Duty*, *Halo*, *Super Mario*, *Fallout*, and so on (the list of "AAA Games" that I enjoy goes on almost endlessly). It was the experiences that I had playing those types of games that got me interested in gaming as well as the video game industry as a business enterprise in the first place. Without those games, I probably would not be as passionate about gaming as I am, and would not be able to draw a comparison between the AAA-space and the more Indie-space in the industry.

This book is *not* about how AAA Developers lack innovation or ability to push the boundaries of the video game industry. In fact, AAA Developers are arguably the most financially capable to create with their multi-million-dollar development and marketing budgets backing their projects.

So, the comparison between the two types of developers is important, but only insofar as it relates to the idea of what it means to be an entrepreneur. My book is about how Indie Game Developers are in fact "entrepreneurs," a fact that is often overlooked when talking about the video game industry. My book seeks to elevate their status by bringing a number of stories of Indie Developers to the forefront and highlight their status as entrepreneurs – pioneers and leaders in the video game industry – and by sharing their stories I hope to inspire future generations of gaming entrepreneurs to chase their dreams.

So, to take my idea and actually apply it, I will provide a few case examples that showcase how, as I will get into greater detail throughout my book, that people in the "Indie Game Development" space or who are tied to being "Indie" are entrepreneurs. The two examples are:

- Nate Mitchell, VP of Product at Oculus VR
- Richard Garriott, Creative Director at Portalarium.

First, there is Nate Mitchell. His perspective admittedly comes more from the perspective as a "Product Guy" as opposed to a traditional video game developer. He represents someone who is in a senior leadership role for one of the most innovative products of 2013-2014. That product being the Oculus Rift, VR Headset — a product that forced Sony and Valve to enter the "Arms Race" that became the Virtual Reality Headset Technology Competition.

As a side note, in the process of interviewing him, I ultimately was able to get an exhibitor's pass at E3 2014 and get a small taste for what it felt like to live in the industry.

But jumping back, Oculus VR was bought by Facebook for a

reported **$2 billion** in the Spring of 2014. They had raised a very successful Kickstarter campaign, one of the more successful Kickstarter campaign and crowded-funded projects in recent history. They were seen as the new innovative technology company on the block. Their mission to bring about a VR experience for the future changed the video game industry for better and for always. After all, *Fallout 4*, one of the most highly rated and popular Role-Playing Games (RPGs) by Bethesda Softworks of all time, was announced at E3 2016 to receive a VR Release.

Although Oculus VR is by no means an Indie Game Development studio, it is very relevant to entrepreneurship and the experiences of Indie Developers. For example, Oculus VR's narrative of crowd funding and success through acquisition speak to various avenues that Indie Developers have access to in terms of promoting their craft. Also, Nate brought a fresh perspective to game development in the way that he communicated the potential of Oculus VR and led groundbreaking efforts to enable game developers to access it and widely encouraged game development using the technology. In many ways, Oculus VR speaks to what it means to be an Independent Game Developer in this day and age.

In the case of Richard Garriott, the pioneer of the Massively Multiplayer Online (MMO) genre, his story is that of a young entrepreneur turned executive producer, then astronaut, and now indie-entrepreneur. His most notable work is *Ultima*, an open world fantasy RPG (Role Playing Game).

He entered into the video game industry at a very young age, in high school actually. Coming from humble beginnings, Richard Garriott quickly started making Dungeons and Dragons-type video games, RPGs and similar type traditional games that we might see nowadays. He quickly found success, and in the process of doing that, he quickly signed onto publishing deals. Ultimately, he founded Origin Systems (est. 1983), a publishing company with his brother. To make a long story short, Electronic Arts (EA) bought Origin Systems for $35 Million in 1992. In 2000, he left Origin to go work at NCsoft, which is arguably most notable for their Guild Wars (MMORPG) series.

Roughly 8 years later, Richard Garriott became an astronaut with NASA, and by 2009-2010, he returned to the video game industry when he founded Portalarium, a video game development studio based out of Austin, TX. Portalarium has developed *Shroud of the Avatar: Forsaken Virtues*, the spiritual successor to the *Ultima* series. Through the use of crowd funding (Kickstarter) and Early Access on Steam, *Shroud of the Avatar* is a game that has strived to change the status quo of what it means to be an online game.

In taking his experiences with the sciences as both an engineer in gaming and as an astronaut, and as a creative visionary, Richard Garriott exemplifies the well-rounded nature of the most successful independent game developers. Richard Garriott has been incredibly successful in his career, which is in large part due to his varied and diverse experiences inside and outside of the video game industry. Future entrepreneurs should take note that gaining varied life experiences will aid your future efforts.

People such as Maxime Beaudoin, a former technical architect for Ubisoft who has worked on both the *Assassin's Creed* and *Prince of Persia* Franchise, independent games development represents an opportunity to take ownership of one's own destiny. While at Ubisoft, Maxime worked with a couple of colleagues on some internal pitches that he hoped might turn into games (they were unsuccessful). When describing what working on those projects felt like, he wrote in a blog post:

> "One of my former colleagues nailed it when he said that I tasted the forbidden fruit. Once you've had that feeling, you can never go back." Maxime reveled in working with talented and motivated people, in a small team environment, while being able to take on a great deal of ownership and major responsibilities. Additionally, Maxime wrote, "Only indie games will let me cover all aspects of the creation process."

Maxime's story shows why it is of the upmost importance for

indie developers to learn and develop a set of skills than can empower them to make the games of future.

In considering the question of "Are Independent Game Developers Entrepreneurs?" to which the answer is "Yes," the question of how Indie Developers fit into the rest of the industry as a whole as a result becomes important to analyze.

Video game developers, whether they are a AAA-developer or an indie developer, grapple with a multitude of issues ranging from the professional to the social/personal. In the case of video games, the three main "social/personal" issues that persist in the industry are that of violent video games, gender bias (and sexism), and racial bias (and racism).

The most culturally relevant issue, considering the United State political landscape as well as dynamics in the video game industry is the issue of gender bias. In the video game industry, there has been a great deal of controversy around gender as it relates to the demographics of the people who work in the industry (and the lack of parity between men and women in the workforce) to how masculinity and femininity is depicted in video games.

Of relevance, I wrote my (high school) senior year Thesis Research Paper on "Gender Bias in the Video Game Industry." I was able to interview Richard Garriott for my senior paper on his perspective of why certain people in the industry thrived or not. In the paper, I examined why certain demographics in the video game industry, especially women, aren't as represented in the video game developer/software engineering side of things relative to men in addition to the issues of hyper-feminization and hyper-masculinization in video games, and a number of other topics related to gender bias and the video game industry. He offered a "chicken versus the egg" perspective of why educationally there haven't been until recently been large numbers of women in the video game development process. This is interesting because the Electronic Software Association (ESA), the trade association for the video game industry, has conducted studies that show that half of all gamers today are women. Moreover, there is the subject of how forcing a gender binary can negatively affect people who identify as transgender.

The issues of gender bias and outright sexism and bigotry play into the video game industry's work culture. The rise of #Gamergate and advocacy of female game developers in the industry are integral to all of this. Gender bias and misogyny are a video game industry issue, both at the AAA level as well as the indie level. Indie developers are uniquely positioned, however, to shine a light on these issues and empower the most marginalized of voices. Significant potential exists for individuals that enter the industry and pioneer gaming solutions to these social issues.

OVERVIEW AND PURPOSE OF THE BOOK

It has been said that 70% of millennials want to be entrepreneurs but *they don't know how to be*. With this book, I want to inspire the next generation of gaming innovators for learn paths to being entrepreneurs. I want to help them understand that an industry just over 40 years old is still poised for continued growth for many decades to come. At over $100 billion in scale. And when you consider that, according to ESA, over 155 million Americans play video games, that there is an average of two gamers per household and that four out of five households own a video game device, one starts to realize that this is a huge and mainstream relevant market. Overlay the fact that half of all gamers are women and few current offerings target this audience, you should see untapped potential.

To help you in this endeavor, I will identify key issues relevant to independent game developers at the end of each chapter. In addition, I will summarize the key insights and lessons learned from the inventors, entrepreneurs, and game developers that you read about in each chapter.

In the simplest of terms, this book is about your empowerment to become an independent game developer and entrepreneur, and, hopefully, **change and redefine** the playing field of the video game industry. I wrote this book because independent game developers do not necessarily see themselves as entrepreneurs, and that is in my view problematic, because they are entrepreneurs. To correctly view yourself as an entrepreneur, not just an independent game developer can be enlightening, liberating and empowering.

As example, I talked to Mark Cooke, the CEO of Shiny Shoe—an independent game developer studio. I asked him, "Do you see yourself an entrepreneur?" At first, he responded, "Maybe." We had to discuss it a bit. He ultimately concluded that, "Yes, he does see himself as an entrepreneur but he doesn't think about."

I wanted to write this book because I wanted to break that down a bit, and show how constantly recognizing that he and Indie Developers like him are entrepreneurs every single day will transform what it means to be an Indie Developer and be a part of the video game industry.

In the case of Mark Cooke, he had gotten that corporate experience and he wanted to forge his own path and do things a little bit differently. Another person I interviewed, Michael Turner, inventor of *Pyclid/We The Players*, he, too, ultimately left his corporate career because he wanted to pursue something in the video game industry.

They both wanted to solve the problems. It was all about this desire to create problems, solve them, to see things in different, unique ways. Michael Turner was someone who tried to break into the industry after leaving a non-gaming industry corporate job. That in a very obvious way is an attribute to Michael's story that makes him an *entrepreneur.*

The casual observer does not realize that the gaming industry is in fact quite democratic. At one level, it's a very hit driven industry like Hollywood where you have major companies that make blockbuster, AAA Games. But, at the same time, you have smaller, more independent teams working on very small projects.

But to reduce the video game industry down to some David and Goliath story does nobody any service. There are so many stories and narratives that define the video game industry, as I have already touched upon and will dive deeper into in this book, that show there is so much beneath the surface that is not really getting talked about.

I believe one of the biggest things people are going to learn from this book is that Independent Game Developers are **entrepreneurs** – and why and how that matters. Moreover, there are many lessons you can learn from industry pioneers and leaders that can make it much easier to break into the industry and make it more likely to accomplish what you want.

It is so easy to say that the video game industry is incredibly simple to break into nowadays with the rise of the App Store and Mobile Gaming as well as the increasing ubiquity of software development platforms (e.g., the Unity Game Engine). But that does not provide much direction or insight at all.

I believe it is invaluable to recognize and appreciate the stories of the shoulders of the giants that you stand on, because they know the video game industry better than anyone else and are therefore powerful resources. Tapping into the wealth of knowledge that industry veterans have can provide great insights about the video game industry, as well as draw attention to the skills and perspectives that have helped people leave a mark on the industry. This book will hopefully provide you with a greater understanding of what it means to be an Indie Developer in the video game industry as well as teach you a lesson or two of entrepreneurship as an Indie Developer.

One of the prevailing stereotypes about people playing video games is that you're going to live in the basement with your parents. There are reasons that type of stereotype has some validity, even if it is not entirely true. Put one way, living in the basement of your parents' house seems like a socially unacceptable thing to do, but from an entrepreneurial perspective it can be incredibly cost effective as an Indie Developer and allow you to save that extra money to get your game off the ground and be more likely to succeed. Because when you are an entrepreneur, like an Indie Developer is, every dollar counts.

There are other lessons people will learn from this book as well. One key lesson involves *risk* and the role it plays in combination with creativity, motivation and payout. The biggest difference between being in a corporate environment versus being in an independent environment is the amount of risk that is taken on by the individual — whether or not you are the person who is bank rolling the team, as the CEO or shareholder, or if you're an individual graphic artist or member of that cohesive unit.

When you're in a corporate environment you have multi-million dollar budgets backing your projects and shareholders who want returns. So, your pressures to succeed and your immediate stability are certifiably different. The lessons of risk that you learn as a result of being in either of those two environments, and your aptitude to take risk on or avoid risk entirely, play into how successful you might or might not be as an Indie Developer.

Being in the video game industry means existing at the intersection of entertainment and technology, and all of the innovations that come from both fields. Being an Independent Game Developer means appreciating that you are creating more than a game, it is a **work of art**, it is an **experience**, if done right it is a work of **true wonder**. Independent Game Developers for these very reasons are entrepreneurs, and their stories and experiences are what define the video game industry every single day.

Jennifer Bullard, Director of Program Management at Querium Corporation, shared with me that it is critical to, "Pick the right battles." Independent developers today are in a unique position, because they have the potential to overtake the video game industry by storm. To share some of the wisdom that Peter Molyneux shared with me, the creative mind behind Fable and more recently the Founder and Creative Director of 22Cans, a UK based independent studio:

> "It's about the iterative process and it's incredibly healthy. Then you go through polish time when you polish that feature, you refine that feature and make it sing. The trouble comes when you reach a point that when you realize no matter what polish you put in, it's going to be wrong and you have to deal with it."

Independent developers are in that iterative process right now, but what they are doing today isn't wrong, because they are challenging the status quo. Independent developers, unlike a developer making a faulty feature in a game, are doing exactly what they are supposed to. Indie developers are polishing their skills and ideas, and as entrepreneurs they are poised to do amazing work.

In the end, it will be the relentless pressure of entrepreneurs that will be the difference between a video game industry focused on creativity and innovation, and an industry that falls behind. I firmly believe that through a greater focus on entrepreneurship, mixed with the appreciation and elevation of artistic design, independent developers will bring about a new age in the video game industry.

PART 1

FITTING IN

CHAPTER 1

THE FIRST VIDEO GAME ENTREPRENEURS

"I thought of doing something radical with a home television set because, after all there about 40 million of them in the United States and maybe another 50 million sets in the rest of the world. I figured maybe if I can attach something to one percent of those sets. Well that looked like a business."

— RALPH BAER ("THE FATHER Of VIDEO GAMES")

CHAPTER FOCUS:

- How and Why the first video game entrepreneurs succeeded

- How the evolution of the video game industry impacts indie developers
- Why mobile and online gaming is changing the video game industry.

In the beginning, Ralph Baer created the first video game console – the Magnavox Odyssey. In September 1966, Ralph Baer envisioned what he called, "video-games," and focused his energy to make that vision a reality.

Ralph Baer's initial concept was "Fox and Hounds" (May 7, 1967). The purpose of the game was to have two spots on a television screen that represented a fox and a hound. The "hound" was tasked with catching the "fox."

Ralph Baer pursued the idea and created a prototype at his employer, Sanders Associates, a military defense-contracting firm based in New Hampshire. Upper-level management saw that the prototype was good and had great promise, and decided to fund a more robust initiative behind the effort. Ralph Baer found a willing and capable colleague in Bill Harrison, another employee at Sanders Associates, and pursued the idea further.

Ralph Baer and Bill Harrison founded a team out of Sanders Associates and created a space known as the "Game Room." From there, they created their first game together. Known as "Firefighter," players were tasked with pumping a lever rapidly to change the color of a "house," that was overlaid on a TV screen from red to blue. And with that simple notion, Ralph Baer and Bill Harrison created the "Pumping Game." The game had received initial criticisms from management for not being "fun enough."

But the "failure" was short lived, for on August 18, 1967, a third man was to join the small team—Bill Rusch—and it changed everything. The triumvirate, by November 1967, had envisioned games that would allow for a third spot on the screen, aka "a ball." By then, what became the most iconic game that defined an industry, "Ping-Pong," or more simply, "Pong," had been born.

Through pure ingenuity, Ralph Baer had invented the first video game console and its initial games. Through talking with many companies on how to launch what at that point was known as the "Brown Box," (the 7th iteration on the initial console design) Magnavox won the contract to manufacture, market, and sell the product. By September 1972, the Magnavox Odyssey was sold in the United States to consumers.

Not to be outdone, Nolan Bushnell, founder of Atari Inc., had seen the Magnavox Odyssey console at a demo and from his own experiences created "Pong." Often cited as the origin story behind the video game industry, *Pong* was not released until months later in November 1972. Although *Pong* popularized the idea, Ralph Baer maintains the title of "Father of Video Games." From there, the rest is history, because from there the video game industry quickly rose and became what it is today – a $100+ billion industry.

That is what is so fascinating: in the very beginning of the video game industry, *there was just one inventor*, Ralph Baer, who had the idea for the video game console, the *Magnavox Odyssey*. His vision ultimately spurred others to capitalize on his success, as many more consoles entered the market. Like with all stories of innovations, especially in the technology space, competition arising from the success of one person's idea (in this case the Magnavox Odyssey) is a recurring theme.

In exploring Ralph Baer's story, one can see how he very much embodies the American Dream. Ralph Baer was born on March 8, 1922, in Germany. Baer was thrown out of school at the age of 16 for being a Jew, due to the rise of Hitler. As a true immigrant and refugee, Baer and his family moved to New York right before World War II began.

He entered into the United States not knowing much English, but he learned to read, write, and speak in English through reading. For Baer, he was able to acclimate and succeed when he got to the United States because he placed an emphasis on reading and education; he championed both reading and education as a means of empowerment and growth until he passed in 2014.

Baer pursued his passions for engineering and problem solving when he joined the U.S. Army, placing into Military Intelligence. And like many Americans, when he finished his service for the Army, he took advantage of the GI Bill and he pursued an education at the American Technical Institute of Technology ATIT) in Chicago, Illinois. From there, he quickly began his career, and, in 1956, he was working at Sanders Associates, the military defense contracting firm where he had his idea for the Magnavox Odyssey.

In the process of doing all of those things, Baer had a stroke of genius that was the basis for the Magnavox Odyssey, which spawned the video game industry. Ralph Baer's story is the American Dream. He took advantage of the opportunities that lay before him. His life story is one of "rags to riches"—the result of both hard work and an entrepreneurial drive that permeated American Culture, especially during that period.

However, with every story of success, there are almost always obstacles that the protagonist of the story must face at some point in their journey. In the case of Ralph Baer, Nolan Bushnell, with the founding of Atari Inc., Mattel, among others capitalized on the Magnavox Odyssey's success and hijacked the founding of the video game industry for their own benefit.

Indeed, many people erroneously associate Nolan Bushnell with the founding of the video game industry. In response, Magnavox filed a number of patent infringement lawsuits, of which Ralph Baer was involved in them all. Magnavox ultimately prevailed in court on all counts and thereby affirmed Ralph Baer's standing as the founder of video games for the ages.

Also during this period, Ralph Baer invented a number of a different toys and game products. Most notably, Ralph Baer created: Simon (1978), Hallmark talking cards (1980s), Chat Mat (1995), Bike Max (1996), and a Hasbro line of talking tools (2002). These toys and inventions further demonstrate Ralph Baer's creative and innovative mindset. Like any entrepreneur, Ralph Baer's life and experiences show the importance of **learning, problem solving, and creation**. His life demonstrates that there is a very strong parallel between entrepreneurship in video game culture and entrepreneurship in traditional startups.

The video game industry evolved over the course of the next two decades. The period of growth laid the foundation for how gamers and developers view the industry as it is today. Its growth and evolution can best be measured by the impacts of three video gaming giants. Richard Garriott, aka "Lord British," and his career represents the early stages of the video game industry; Christopher Weaver, the founder of Bethesda

Softworks, exemplifies the rise of major corporations in the industry; and Gordon Walton, a video game developer and executive producer. Each of those industry leaders represents the return to the industry's entrepreneurial roots that began with Ralph Baer, as I discuss below.

RICHARD GARRIOTT: A MAJOR SHIFT IN THE VIDEO GAME INDUSTRY

Richard Garriott began writing (computer) video games in 1974. His first projects were role-playing experiences based primarily on Dungeons & Dragons. Garriott made 28 different D&D games, but he found the most success with his 28th game.

The game's development, which lasted 1979-1980, took advantage of the Apple II's introduction of graphics. He decided to rename the game "*Akalabeth*: (World of Doom)." In talking about how he came up with the name he said that *Akalabeth* was, "a word that I thought I had made up from scratch, however I am very confident now in hindsight that it's virtually the same as one of the chapters in JRR Tolkien's The Lord of the Rings, spelled a little bit differently. It's from where I got the inspiration unwittingly." The name Origin makes sense considering Garriott's passion for medieval fantasy.

After finishing the game in 1980, Garriott decided to self-publish the game and sell the game himself. As this was happening,

Akalabeth received attention from a publishing company, California Pacific, and the company signed Richard Garriott on to publish the game. Because of *Akalabeth's* success Richard Garriott used the royalties that he earned to create his most notable title – *Ultima*. On the subject of *Ultima* Richard Garriott said, "*Ultima* began as the first product I developed intending it to be played by gamers."

Without any peers or predecessors to base his work off of, Richard Garriott was defining the role-playing game genre for computer gaming; this all happened by about 1981. As a result, most role-playing games (RPGs) of today are rooted in the Dungeons & Dragons variants that Richard Garriott made. In thinking about making a more RPG-focused game, or any genre of game more generally, it is important to hone in on original concepts that make the game fun while at the same time pushing the envelope in some way.

By 1983, Richard Garriott founded the video game development company Origin Systems with his brother Robert Garriott in Austin, Texas. It was at Origin Systems where Richard Garriott worked to make *Ultima* the highly-acclaimed gaming series that many gamers know of today; Origin Systems is also known as the company behind the famed *Wing Commander* series. Within 10 years, in September 1992, Electronic Arts (EA), acquired Origin Systems for a reported $35 Million.

Through his visionary work, Richard Garriott in 1997 coined the term massively multiplayer online role-playing game (MMORPG) and pioneered the MMO genre. As a shining example of the success some people found in the video game industry's early days, Richard Garriott redefined that gaming not only a one-on-one or a with-a-friend experience, but that it quickly became an online experience as well. This was in no small part due to the fact that the Internet was first invented in the 1980s and 1990s.

In many ways, even in the early days of video game industry, video games became most successful when they were created at the intersection of technology and entertainment. Richard Garriott's diverse backgrounds and experiences, as an astronaut and a constant student of many different disciplines, also play an integral role in his success.

CHRISTOPHER WEAVER: MAJOR PUBLISHING COMPANIES CONTROL THE GAME

Christopher Weaver entered the video game industry in the 1980s, which was when major publishing companies started their rise to prominence. Arguably the rise of these developers and the role of publishers was made possible by the recession that hit the video game industry from 1983 to 1985. The "North American video game industry crash of 1983" was a result of the over-saturation of the market by opportunistic entrants coupled with chronic inflation plaguing the U.S. Economy.

Activision Inc. was founded in 1979 and Electronic Arts (EA) was founded in 1982. Almost by accident, Christopher Weaver founded the video game developer and publisher Bethesda Softworks in 1986, selling the first video game that made use of a real-time physics engine. That game was "Gridiron!" Because of this innovation, EA hired Bethesda in order to make the first game in the John Madden Football series, more commonly known as "Madden NFL" the most popular sports video game in history.

Today, when gamers think of Bethesda Softworks they think of Elder Scrolls and Fallout, which are two of the biggest and most popular Role-playing Game (RPG) series in gaming culture. Based out of Bethesda, Maryland, Christopher Weaver created one of the most iconic, premier video game publishing companies that gamers know and love. Weaver co-founded ZeniMax Media in 1999, to expand its reach and solidify Bethesda's renowned status on a larger level.

Weaver brought in Robert Altman to run ZeniMax so he could act as Chief Technology Officer (CTO) and concentrate on technology. But like Steve Jobs and John Scully, Altman and Weaver did not get along and Altman maneuvered to get Weaver out of the company he founded. Weaver later sued the company for breach of contract. The Court of Special Appeals (in Maryland) ruled in Weaver's favor and, in the end, the parties settled. Still one of its largest private stockholders, Weaver left ZeniMax to teach and continues to teach at MIT and is also a Visiting Professor of Computational Media at Wesleyan University. He has an abundance of academic honors and technical awards that recognize his career and contributions to technology. In 2016 Weaver was appointed a Distinguished Research Scholar at the Smithsonian and chosen to create the Smithsonian's Videogame Pioneers Archive at its inaugural Director.

But what is really fascinating about Weaver's career as it relates to the video game industry is the fact that he, along with many others who had no initial training in making videos games, play a major role in the rise of prominence of the major publishing companies that exist in the industry today. By creating Bethesda Softworks and producing the Elder Scrolls, Weaver's company has become the reference standard by which all other RPGs are measured. Additionally, by expanding its purview, through ZeniMax, Weaver position Bethesda Softworks to become a titan in the industry. In comparison to Richard Garriott's career from 1974-2000, Christopher Weaver's career exemplifies how the video game industry has experienced a tectonic shift from individuals creating games to large-scale enterprises encompassing hundreds of people and many millions of dollars.

Gordon Walton: The Height of MMORPGs and the Return to Indie Gaming

Gordon Walton has been a part of the video game industry since 1978. In the video game industry, Gordon Walton is a true renaissance man. With experience as an executive producer working on games such as *Ultima Online* (2000-2001) at Origin Systems, *The Sims* (2003) at Maxis under EA, *Star Wars: Galaxies* (2004) at Sony Online Entertainment (SOE), and *Star Wars: The Old Republic* (2011) at BioWare Austin, Gordon Walton knows a great deal about the MMO genre and online gaming. Each of these games, which were all published by major publishing companies, had an impact and influence on the industry was immense.

Given this track record of success, Gordon Walton's decision to leave the more corporate and well-established culture of working at Playdom in 2013, after Disney Interactive had acquired it in 2010 for $763.2 million, might seem surprising. As Gordon explained his decision:

> "I enjoyed programming. I would have done it even if I wasn't getting published. I was interested in creating things, even though I had no idea if they would turn into anything beyond that. It was challenging, we were working with tiny amounts of memory and pretty crappy languages but that is part of what programming is … solving puzzles. I enjoyed solving puzzles."

subject areas, because that was what allowed him to think critically about any given problem.

Gordon loved to solve problems, though, because he loved learning new and different things. Much like Ralph Baer, Gordon appreciated the importance of learning and understanding of a variety of ideas and concepts from different

Like Richard Garriott, who re-entered the video game industry in 2010, Gordon Walton was going back to his roots as an inde-pendent game developer and embracing his entrepreneurial personality. Gordon Walton is a successful and well-respected video game developer, which makes his decision all the more meaningful. This decision draws to the forefront how in the video game industry there is a growing desire by many devel-opers and gamers alike to go back to Indie Game Development.

MOBILE GAMING IS A DEMOCRATIZING FORCE IN THE VIDEO GAME INDUSTRY

Now there are many innovators and pioneers in the video game industry who have taken Ralph Baer's work and built on it, expanded it, and taken it to a new level of excitement and innovation. The result of these innovations has meant that the video game industry has evolved from a budding enterprise to become as massive and all-encompassing as Hollywood and Music.

With the rise of the iPhone and the advent of the App Store, mobile gaming has allowed anyone with passion and the initiative to make a game. David Helgason, co-founder of Unity Technologies, a tech-startup whose game development platform (Unity) has revolutionized game design through democratization believes that as technology has prolifer-ated, the potential for the video game industry to grow and become even more diverse in terms people making games, people playing games, and the games getting made will be a net benefit for everyone.

David, speaking on Unity, said, "We fell in love with the tool that we made for ourselves and realized that tool might have a big impact on the industry and we might be able to change the industry. It's crazy to think but the fact that we believed we could do that ended up guiding us to actually try and eventually succeed." The belief that anyone who has a love for what they are doing has the power to change the indus-try speaks to the tectonic shift that the video game industry has experienced. As technology continues to evolve, which it seems to do at an increasing rate, with the introduction of virtual reality, augmented reality, mobile gaming, and more, the video game industry will never be the same. To quote Gordon Walton:

> "The future of video games is easy: it's change. If you think about where games have been all along, we have always been an entertainment medium, so we ride in

the place with high tech and consumer trends, which are both changing very fast and so we ride both of those. So, it's not like we are just in the high-tech industry or we are just in the entertainment industry, we're in both. It's not additive, it's more multiplicative, and so it's really chal-lenging to hit the right mark."

The telling part about what Gordon is stressing is that it is important to be nimble and adapt to change, because in the video game industry it can come out of nowhere at any time.

In order to deal with this level of change, Ralph Baer, Rich-ard Garriott, and Gordon Walton, all stressed through their life experiences and in what they have said that it is vital to constantly learn and solve problems in order to succeed. Engineering and software development backgrounds might seem like the norm in the video game industry, but a princi-ple concern, more than anything else, is the ability to solve problems in a variety of different ways. The video game industry, although it is far beyond what Ralph Baer had originally created with the invention of the Magnavox Odyssey, is as inventive, creative, and dynamic just as Ralph was. Which is saying a great deal. Although there are many entrepreneurs who have shaped the video game industry and brought fun and joy to hundreds of millions of people, one cannot help but be reminded of the powerful impact that just *one* man, Ralph Baer, who started it all.

KEY INSIGHTS AND TAKEAWAY LESSONS

- Today we often think that only big companies (AAA) launch video games, but the reality is this industry has largely been created by entrepreneurs and many of your favorite games were started by indie developers
- There is a perception that to be an entrepreneur in the video game industry you need to be a programmer or an engineer, but the truth is that the most successful people have a well-rounded background (e.g., education/ professional/etc.)
- To identify future growth streams, become educated about the history of the industry, how new innovations at the time carved out new growth waves (e.g., RPGs, the rise of publishers, MMOs, online gaming)
- With the rise of technology (especially mobile gaming), almost anyone can make a video game and enter the industry

ADDITIONAL INDUSTRY VETERAN PERSPECTIVE:

"Start small. If you're a programmer, clone something like pong to understand the basics of game development. Then put your own twist on it by changing the design in a subtle or not-so-subtle way. Build up from these basics and don't try to build an MMORPG at the start. It will just discourage you."

— MARK COOKE (CEO, SHINY SHOE)

"The industry is really about pushing the technology in some way and then combine that with entertainment and storytelling and fun."

— JOHN ERSKINE (VP OF PUBLISHING,

CLOUD IMPERIUM GAMES)

CHAPTER 2

INDEPENDENT GAMING: COMPETING IN A CHANGING LANDSCAPE

"Game companies are like a rollercoaster ride, you are either growing or shrinking, you are almost never just staying the same."

— JOHN ERSKINE (VP OF PUBLISHING,
CLOUD IMPERIUM GAMES)

CHAPTER FOCUS:

- Overview of the Industry Landscape as it relates to AAA-gaming
- Examination of how the Video Game Industry acts like Hollywood

- Analysis of the Strengths and Weaknesses of AAA-gaming and where Independent Game Developers can compete
- Staying up to date on the video game industry (in the future)

To quote Steve Jobs, "Picasso had a saying — 'good artists copy; *great artists steal*' — and we have always been shameless about stealing great ideas." Steve Jobs' philosophy was about taking other people's impressive work and creating even more meaningful innovations from original inspiration. That philosophy is how the hit game *Minecraft* came to be. When Markus "Notch" Persson originally made the game, he based it off of someone else's work — which all happened by chance.

As the story goes, Markus played a game called *Infiniminer* in the spring of 2009, and he called indie developer Zachary Barth's work on the game "pure genius." Unfortunately, (or fortunately, depending on your perspective) *Infiniminer's* source code was leaked online and the game's chances of becoming a breakout died. As a result of the leak, though, a curious thing happened: programmers and gamers alike took the until-recently private source code and created their own individual versions of the game. Other independent game developers were able to make Infiniminer what they wanted it to be. While this was terrible for Barth, it was a great opportunity for the larger community to develop multiple concurrent versions of the same game.

The problem was, of course, that when they made hundreds of new games, they were all incompatible, so nobody could play with each other. Since the original game was intended to be multiplayer, this was clearly problematic. Barth realized that he had an opportunity to turn lemons into lemonade, and made a decision: he would upload the original game online as open source code, so people could take that version and modify as they wished. He did so knowing that Infiniminer would never truly be an online game as had intended, but he could turn individual adversity into advantage for the whole community.

But since the original release of *Minecraft* in 2009, Markus has set the gold standard of gaming development: from the open documentation of the development process to the dialogue he fostered with the *Minecraft* community, Markus rewrote the rules of what it meant to be a great video game developer. From 2009 to 2016, *Minecraft* became a juggernaut in video game culture. Now there is the MineCon event (a convention centered around all things *Minecraft*). As of July 2016, it had a reported 100 million copies sold worldwide on a multitude of platforms (PC, console, and mobile alike). Most of all, Markus sold his company Mojang and *Minecraft* along with it for a reported $2.5 Billion in 2014.

Markus and his work on *Minecraft* represents one of the many moments in recent history where the video game industry has begun to see a major shift in terms of how it operates. And the video game industry does not show any signs of slowing down. In fact, the pace these shifts will only increase in speed, if the recent history is any indication.

When talking about a changing landscape in the video game industry, Markus' work has dramatically changed video game development. It is essential to understand though how that fits into an industry shaped by major publishers and AAA-gaming. Markus is an independent video game developer, but his work influence demands a re-evaluation of the video game industry landscape. Many gamers, when they talk about gaming place a great deal of emphasis on major publishing companies and AAA-Development Studios, which have traditionally dominated the video game space. The video game industry, in the AAA space, is a massively complex entity that merits its own examination. And in order to fully appreciate the impact of *Minecraft* as it relates to gaming, it is important to first understand the video game industry landscape. The video game industry brings in $100 Billion annually, whereas other entertainment industries are smaller in terms of revenues: Books ($24 Billion), Music ($15 Billion), and Hollywood ($38 Billion).

In breaking down AAA-Gaming, a distinction needs to be made between publishers and developers. A typical gamer knows that a developer is a software developer who specializes in video game development – they make the games – and that a publisher manufactures, markets, and distributes the games. This is how Hollywood operates. Just as Walt Disney Pictures and Pixar Animation Studios are the production companies behind *Inside Out* (2015), which was distributed by Walt Disney Studios Motion Pictures, BioWare is the video game development studio behind *Mass Effect 3* (2012), which was published by Electronic Arts (EA).

It is worth drawing a comparison between the video game industry and Hollywood because it speaks to how the video game industry is an industry geared towards entertainment and therefore in a lot of ways operates as an industry. The video game industry is also technologically oriented, because of the nature of video games, but although video game companies are tech companies, they are not solely focused on technology – they thrive at the **intersection** of technology and entertainment where *innovation* is most present.

In evaluating the landscape of the video game industry, there are three major video game publishers worth talking about: Activision, EA, and Ubisoft. There is a litany of major video game publisher companies, as well as a number of mid-size publisher companies. But in considering the landscape of the video game industry, Activision, EA, and Ubisoft are the most notable in terms of the video games that they publish.

Activision is most commonly known as Activision Blizzard. Activision Blizzard, formerly known as Activision Inc., became the company that it is today as a result of a merger after Vivendi SA bought Activision Inc. in 2008. As a result of the merger, and Activision Blizzard's buyout from Vivendi in 2013 for a reported $5.83 Billion, Activision Blizzard became the company that gamers know of today. Activision Blizzard owns Activision, Blizzard Entertainment, Major League Gaming, Activision Blizzard Studios, and King Digital Entertainment.

Activision Blizzard is known for the famous video game franchises such as *Call of Duty*, *Destiny*, *Overwatch*, *World of Warcraft*, and *Candy Crush Saga*. As a result, Activision Blizzard is a company known for having megabrands that they leverage with numerous game releases within a megabrand umbrella. The company is known for setting records that surpass Hollywood ticket sale revenues, and that is because of their constant pursuit of acquiring and publishing such commercially successful gaming brands:

- King Digital Entertainment originally developed *Candy Crush Saga* and was acquired by Activision for $5.9 billion dollars in February of 2016
- Activision Blizzard also bought Major League Gaming, the premier eSports organizations, in January 2016
- *World of Warcraft* (2004-Present) is hailed as one of the most successful MMORPGs of all time

- The *Call of Duty* franchise, especially with the Modern War-fare trilogy, is known for breaking blockbuster movie records comparable to James Cameron's Avatar (2009), on the order of $1 Billion
- *Destiny*, when it was released in 2014, became known as the most successful new gaming franchise launch with over $500 Million shipped to retailers worldwide at launch
- *Overwatch* (2016), the latest new IP by Blizzard Entertainment, was awarded Game of the Year at The Game Awards 2016

Activision Blizzard's reputation as one of the biggest video game publishers and most well respected (if not necessarily by all gamers) in the industry is understandable. Therefore, when considering the magnitude and impact of major video game publishers, it is worth recognizing the apt comparison between the video game industry and Hollywood. Video game movie adaptations, regardless of how critically acclaimed or commercially successful they may be, depending on the case, represent another reason why the industry is a force to be reckoned with.

To not make the comparison would dismiss how video games, as a business, is not only highly profitable but also relevant in terms of cultural value. *Call of Duty*, one of Activision Blizzard's most successful video game franchises, has entertain-ment value and revenue potential comparable to a Marvel film or the *Fast & Furious* franchise. *Call of Duty* is representative of the **Blockbuster** action sequences that typify **AAA-games** and games development in the video game industry. But in making that comparison, it becomes clear that especially with Activision Blizzard, that games that get published at the AAA-level are directed towards the same audiences and are similar in gameplay experiences. *Call of Duty* and *Destiny*, which are both published by Activision Blizzard, although they are *different* IPs, are in reality more similar than one might think: they are both first person shooters, both place a strong emphasis on the social and online experiences, both are recognized for their action sequences, and both games are made by developers with phenomenal pedigrees; *Destiny* by Bungie, the developer behind the *Halo Series* and *Call of Duty* by Infinity Ward, Treyarch, or Sledgehammer games depending on the year and the franchise's development cycle between the development studios.

For anyone who has an understanding of the video game industry, this is true for both EA and Ubisoft, but on slightly different genres than Activision Blizzard, it is clear that the most popular games are made in a specific subset of genres. This can be good in that there is a plethora of game choices from people who like shooter, sports, or more action oriented games, but at the same time it **limits** the number of game experiences out there that people can play.

Independent developers, however, because they are not tied

to making big-budget games, can make more varied games. In fact, that is actually what has allowed a number of indie developers to succeed. *Minecraft*, a sandbox game where players simply make things, might at first seem like a niche game, but as of July 2016, over 100 million copies have been sold worldwide. So, although *Minecraft* might seem *niche*, because it is not a first-person shooter (FPS) or a sports game, because it was a compelling and unique game that went against the norms of AAA games, the game was able to succeed and become a cultural icon. Therefore, it is useful to consider when making a game what type of experience you are setting out create, because sometimes the outside of the box indie games, like *Minecraft*, can do just as well if not better than their AAA counterparts.

Because a strong of AAA games are comparable to Blockbuster Movies, there is a fair comparison to be made in terms of set pieces versus storytelling. Call of Duty, one of the most commercially successful first-person shooter (FPS) games of all time, is a game that has been criticized for telling the same repetitive story almost every year without fail. In the final moments of every Call of Duty, the player character and a close ally fight the antagonist. As the structure of the finale always plays out: the ally is overpowered and left unconscious by the antagonist, the player takes on the antagonist one-on-one, the player is on the verge of being killed by the enemy, the ally saves the player in some way (an ex machina), and finally as the ally is fighting the antagonist the player through some miraculous set of circumstances is able to kill and defeat the antagonist. As a result of these parallels and seemingly lack of originality in a number of AAA games (like Call of Duty), which are still nevertheless fun to play, massive and dynamic set pieces arguably take priority over original and engaging storytelling.

Therefore, as an independent game developer, much like an indie filmmaker in Hollywood, it is important to consider the right balance between set pieces and storytelling, because striking the right balance will make the difference between being a stereotypical, annualized released game and a unique gaming experience. Both games can be great in their own ways, but the more compelling stories often last longer with and have a deeper impact on the people that play those games.

Elon Musk, a prolific entrepreneur and CEO of both SpaceX and Tesla Motors, and Sam Altman (President, Y Combinator) in January 2017 dialogued about storytelling in video games. Both Elon Musk and Sam Altman are gamers at heart, and deeply enjoy both the Activision Blizzard game, *Overwatch* (2016); one of Elon Musk's all-time favorite games is *Deus Ex* (2000). On the subject, Elon Musk said:

"I think that [storytelling's] really neglected. That's the

criticism I've heard of the latest *Deus Ex*, is that the storytelling is kind of lame."

In line with this idea, Sam Altman added to the conversation:

"As games have become more like the replacement for the NFL, I think the storytelling just gets generally neglected … so it's especially striking to play one that was, like, absolutely cinematic."

Elon Musk furthered the contrast between cinematic gaming experiences and storytelling by saying:

"Some of the oldest games, the graphics and sound were terrible, so they had to rely on storytelling."

In sum, storytelling as a means to further enrich a gaming experience is important to making great games. *The Last of Us* (2013) is an example that Sam Altman pointed to in their conversation of a game that has found the right balance between storytelling and cinematic experiences. In the entrepreneurial space, people often joke that when Elon Musk says something people jump at his words and listen intently. In this particular instance, although he is not a game developer, Elon Musk and Sam Altman, as gamers, make a compelling case on how a developer can make video games better. As a means of differentiation between other independent games and AAA games, storytelling is but one way to accomplish this goal.

Like any company at the forefront of their industry, Activision Blizzard has a CEO, Bobby Kotick, who leads the company towards greatness. Bobby Kotick, in addition to his role as CEO of Activision Blizzard, is also on the Board of Directors at The Coca-Cola Company. The truly astounding part about Bobby Kotick as CEO of Activision Blizzard is that he has been the company's **CEO for 25 years**. This is a feat in of itself, because the average tenure of a CEO at a company is 4.6 years. Moreover after, Larry Ellison, co-Founder of Oracle Corporation (the makers of Java), stepped down as CEO of Oracle in 2014, Bobby Kotick became the longest standing CEO at a Fortune 500 company. This breaks any norms or conceptions of business that many people might have, especially about the video game industry. More than that, Bobby Kotick's tenure speaks to the corporate culture that thrives at Activision Blizzard. The only place you might see a similar type of story take place is in Hollywood, where companies are steeped in a culture of leadership that does not experience much turnover unless absolutely necessary. But that relates to the dynamics of Bobby Kotick is as the leader of Activision Blizzard. Thus, Activision Blizzard plays a critical role as a major video game publisher in the industry.

EA is the colloquial name for Electronic Arts, another major video game publisher in the industry. They're also a major player in the industry, but they stand out as a company and an organization for a myriad of different reasons. First and foremost, consumers ranked EA as one of the worst companies in the United States in 2012 and 2013 according to Consumerist. EA attained this title alongside companies such as Comcast, Bank of America, Monsanto, Halliburton, Countrywide Financial, and Wal-Mart. In 2012, the runner-up to EA was Bank of America, and AT&T and Wal-Mart tied for third place. In 2013, Bank of America was the runner-up again, with Comcast in third place. Comcast took the title as "Worst Company in America" in 2014 arguably because EA responded and changed its marketing strategy. Every year there a number of gamers who complain about the latest iteration of *Call of Duty* being the worst thing to happen to gaming, but EA took precedence above all of that a received this inauspicious honors of "Worst Company in America" two years in a row. The very fact that consumers (**gamers**) felt such a visceral negative opinion towards EA highlights how the video game industry rivals many Fortune 500 companies in relevance to daily life.

EA pioneered using business principles to influence video games development. Most notably, EA led the charge in the introduction of season passes, where gamers pay an upfront fee in order to receive *"extra content,"* known as Downloadable Content (DLC) without having to pay individually upon each DLC release. This has become increasingly problematic from the standpoint that gamers believe, and understandably so, that companies such as EA are creating pay walls that prevent access to game content that perhaps should have been made available with the rest of the game at launch. This particular strategy by EA to employ DLC and in-game micro-transactions more generally has elevated EA's status as a competitive business and player in the video game industry.

EA also has a strong influence as a publisher in the video game industry. Since the company's founding in 1982, EA has operated on a model centered on creating partnerships with studios and through direct ownership of game development studios. Specifically, EA is known for having a branched company structure: EA Games, EA Sports, EA Maxis, and EA All Play. EA Games is the EA Label responsible for the more action-oriented, role playing, racing and combat games. The two most noteworthy studios under the EA Games Label are DICE and BioWare. DICE is known for:

- The *Battlefield* Franchise
- The reboot of Star Wars Battlefront
- The *Mirror's Edge* series

BioWare is the studio behind EA's role-playing game titles, most especially:

- *Star Wars: Knights of the Old Republic* (RPG)

- Star Wars: The Old Republic (an MMO based on the RPG series)
- The *Mass Effect* Saga
- The Dragon's Age series

EA Sports is the EA Label that represents every EA sports title. Some of the EA Sports Branded games include (but are not limited to):

- *Madden NFL*, which was originally created under an EA contract by Bethesda Softworks
- *FIFA Football*
- *NCAA Branded Games (including NCAA Basketball* and *NCAA Football)*
- *Tiger Woods PGA Tour*
- *NHL Hockey*, among others

EA Maxis is the brand behind the famous *The Sims Series, Sims City,* and *Spore* (all created by the visionary Will Wright). The main point being, EA is formidable in the video game industry and was justly considered the fourth largest video game company in 2014, behind Tencent, Sony, and Microsoft.

EA has a similar big budget AAA-games development culture to Activision Blizzard, but as a company EA is most certainly different. EA is known as a company that places the shareholder bottom line above innovation. This is a major reason behind why gamers view EA as negatively as they do.

At the same time, the company's goal is to be a successful company that benefits shareholders which means that EA has done a great deal in terms of creating a formidable stake in the industry. EA currently holds the rights to create all Star Wars content through 2023, a deal they made with Disney after Disney bought LucasFilm in 2012. In going back to the Hollywood comparison, EA, much like Disney does in Hollywood, controls Star Wars and some of the most profitable licenses of the industry. Moreover, EA acquired Origin Systems, which was founded by Richard Garriott, in 1992; EA shut down Origin Systems in 2004.

Also, in response to the criticisms that the company has faced, EA is trying to restore a culture of innovation in a corporate setting. After a great deal of planning, at the Electronic Entertainment Expo (E3 2016), the premier annual showcase event for the video game industry, EA unveiled EA Originals. The initiative is based on the notion that gamers want to play Indie Games, and EA believes that EA Originals is the answer. EA Originals represents a partnership between independent game developers and EA where EA has agreed to partner with a select number of independent game developers to market, publish, and distribute their games. At E3 2015, EA announced their very first Indie Game partnership, the product of which is a game called *Unravel*, a yarn-based platformer game that was developed by the Swedish independent game developer, ColdWood Interactive. The most telling impact of

EA Originals is that there is no sign of the initiative stopping any time soon.

With all of this in mind, EA, through the intentional desire to benefit the shareholder bottom-line, found value in promoting a culture of innovation. These decisions, among others, catapulted EA to become the top video game publisher in 2014, which as a result changed the landscape of the video game industry. There might be a subset of the gamer population that holds distrust towards EA, because EA in their minds represents the epitome of "evil corporations," but it is difficult to argue the impact EA has had on the video game industry. EA pioneered the use of DLC and paid content, brought back *Star Wars Battlefront* into the hands of gamers (2015), is the leader in sports gaming (*Madden NFL, FIFA, NHL Hockey*), and helped lead the charge in partnering with independent game developers. All of those things are considered commonplace to gamers in the 21st century. Therefore, although competing against AAA companies is often the norm, the circumstances are not always black and white, so it comes down to the priorities of a given independent developer to grapple with how to perceive publishing companies given this landscape.

Then there is Ubisoft, more formally known as Ubisoft Entertainment SA. Ubisoft is known for their model of games releasing on an annually, having multiple development studios across the world work on their games (resulting in 24/7 development), and pushing the boundaries of open-world and always online gaming. Some of Ubisoft's top gaming brands include:

- *Assassin's Creed*
- *Tom Clancy Games (Splinter Cell, Rainbow Six, Ghost Recon)*
- *Watch Dogs*
- *Far Cry*
- *Just Dance*

To make a comparison to Hollywood, Ubisoft represents the part of Hollywood that thinks everything must be a sequel and everything must be a franchise. The *Assassin's Creed* series, Ubisoft's flagship gaming IP, since *Assassin's Creed II* was released in 2009, has seen an annualized release every single year up until 2016. The reason Ubisoft decided to have its studios miss a 2016 release and delay until 2017 was due to the concerns of "***series fatigue***" brought on by the inability to bring about cutting-edge innovations to the series because the development schedule was not flexible.

As a result of Ubisoft's innovations in the video game industry, games are becoming increasingly "**always online**", which means that even if the game is supposedly single-player, the game still requires an internet connection. Some have hailed the online multiplayer focus as innovative and a potent tool to drive video game experiences as well as sales numbers, but it has also meant the decline of single-player only experiences. There are still a good number of single-player only or single-player and multi-player games, but the trend has been towards going online. Independent game developers have found this and been able to capitalize on this niche, because making online focused games is an expensive endeavor in of itself. Because these games are becoming increasingly expensive to make, fewer new IP games every year can be made because of the risk and uncertainty associated with launching a new IP. For video games development, it has meant that games are increasingly be sold *"incomplete,"* as either unfinished products that include problems that have to be fixed via a patch and, or requiring DLC to be bought in order to enjoy the full experience of the game. Additionally, this has meant that the games that do get made are usually made on an annual basis, with a 2-3-year development cycle, in an attempt to maximize value and drive sales numbers.

The annualized nature of Ubisoft's games, especially for *Assassin's Creed*, was a winning strategy for Ubisoft until *Assassin's Creed* Unity in 2014 released to mixed reviews and a less than stellar launch. Ubisoft found this to be successful because they forced the developers for their games to become increasingly specialized during the game development process. Ubisoft, much like Ford with the release of the Model T in the early 1900s, endorses a policy of "Taylorism" where individual developers would become the specialist in a given field (e.g., making lampposts). Considering there are usually hundreds if not a couple thousand people working on a single *Assassin's Creed* game at any one time, this strategy practically guarantees success until concerns of quality assurance are raised.

In addition to the fact that having AAA developers make games in a 24/7 culture has created burnout within the video game industry, the strategy has also stretched Ubisoft quite thin. Since October 2015, Vivendi, the company, which had previously owned Activision Blizzard, has actively pursued an ownership stake in Ubisoft. This matters because Ubisoft is a family run company. The Guillemot family founded Ubisoft in 1986, and Ubisoft has been family owned and operated ever since with Yves Guillemot as CEO. Gameloft, a sister company to Ubisoft focused on mobile gaming, was founded in 2000 by Michel Guillemot. To make matters more complicated, in June 2016, Vivendi completed a successful hostile takeover. Vivendi leadership has claimed that they do not want to take control of Ubisoft, but Vivendi's growing stake in the company says otherwise. Considering the impact Vivendi had on Activision and Blizzard Entertainment to form Activision Blizzard, and Ubisoft's own impact on the video game industry, the landscape of the video game industry is sure to change in some way before Vivendi gives up its stake in Ubisoft. The significance of this cannot be overstated. If Vivendi successfully took over Ubisoft and perhaps merged

Gameloft and Ubisoft before ultimately getting bought out by the Guillemot family, just as Activision Blizzard did with Vivendi in 2013, one less company would play a role in the video game industry landscape.

As an independent developer it is important to keep in mind the pressures that exist at the higher levels of the video game industry, because although these companies might represent competition or potential partners, depending on the perspective taken, what happens to them reverberates throughout the video game industry. If Ubisoft and Gameloft were to merge in a buyout from Vivendi, the strategies of both Activision Blizzard and EA would surely change, and it is foreseeable that they could affect their dealings with independent developers.

The video game industry landscape has been forged and defined by many video game publishers, but Activision Blizzard, EA, and Ubisoft make up the vast majority of the landscape relative to every other company. As a result of the consolidation in the video game industry in terms of company mergers and acquisitions, the video game industry is looking more like Hollywood every single year. These companies are beginning to make fewer bigger bets in the video games that agree to publish. In considering *Call of Duty*, *Madden NFL*, and *Assassin's Creed*, as games by their respective publishers, they are all annualized games, they all rake in millions if not billions of dollars upon release, and they are becoming the norm for AAA-gaming and major video game publishers. These results appease shareholders, and gamers do not have much choice other than to buy these games if they want to experience AAA-gaming, as it exists today.

The video game industry is becoming all the more oriented towards always online, increasingly casual, and fast-paced gaming. As the major video game publishers change the landscape of the video game industry, by making fewer bigger bets. As the video game industry has become more centered on this landscape, independent game developers have received more attention and focus from gamers, critics, and publishers alike. Independent game developers in recent years, and especially so in 2016, have found that their niche is expanding. And as this niche expands, it becomes all the more vital to recognize who independent game developers are, how they relate to the video game industry, and the impact that they might have on the video game industry in the next five to ten, possibly even twenty years from now.

Given that the video game industry experiences constant change, it is important to figure out the best ways to stay up to date and informed. Some key resources to consider are new media outlets such as Game Informer, Kotaku, GameSpot, and Polygon. Most notably, Gamastutra is a great website to get the latest information from the developer-facing side on the video game industry. It is also important to follow influencers in the video game industry, from the top developers and their studios, or gaming icons such as Larry Hryb, Director of Programming for Xbox Live, Geoff Keighley, a gaming journalist and icon who both creating and hosting The Game Awards after the Spike Video Game Awards ended, as well as other such people.

KEY INSIGHTS AND TAKEAWAY LESSONS

- The video game industry **operates** like <u>Hollywood</u>
  - Anyone with the initiative and a passion can try to break into the industry, but it requires hard work and experience to be successful.
- The video game industry is at the intersection of technology and entertainment, is innovative, and is constantly changing
  - It is important to be able to adapt to and better yet anticipate, the ever changing landscape if you want to compete.
- AAA gaming is becoming increasingly oriented towards experiences that are: Blockbuster, online-centric, focused on specific genres (e.g., sports, shooters, action-oriented), which means indie developers should consider wisely before making games in these genres.
- AAA gaming is experiencing a crisis of innovation in that the consolidation in the industry means fewer gaming experiences are being offered to different gaming interests – this is an opportunity to make games that fill those niches
  - Find the right *balance* between **Set Pieces** and **Storytelling**

- Major publishing companies are always seeking new and unique winning strategies—in particular, partnering with and sponsoring some indie developers – this is an opportunity to make a name for yourself
  - But be careful and do not end up like *No Man's Sky* by Hello Games

ADDITIONAL INDUSTRY VETERAN PERSPECTIVE:

"We founded Lionhead with the precept of attempting to do innovation games that others wouldn't dare to do. There is a distrust of innovation that larger corporations have. It's very hard, you say this line, it's like nothing that ever came before. So they try to see through the fog of what an idea is, if they can't get their hands on it. We founded ourselves upon let's have a great idea, let's get a great team together and let's make a great product for people that we feel are starved for innovation."

— PETER MOLYNEUX (FOUNDER, LIONHEAD STUDIOS AND 22CANS)

"Be prepared to start at the bottom and learn as much as you can from every position as you gain experience and greater opportunities."

— JOHN ERSKINE (VP OF PUBLISHING, CLOUD IMPERIUM GAMES)

CHAPTER 3

VIDEO GAME INDUSTRY WEAKNESSES: AN INDEPENDENT GAMING OPPORTUNITY

———

"I think you can easily be working in games instead with the goal of making something meaningful, something that where the goal is like primarily to express yourselves with the mediums and create something that's delightful and wonderful, whatever."

— DAVID HELGASON (CO-FOUNDER, UNITY TECHNOLOGIES)

CHAPTER FOCUS:

- Examination of the "Myths" of the Industry and Gaming Culture and why some ring true more than others
- How the Minefields of Gaming can be problematic for AAA Games, but might be an Opportunity for Independent Developers
- Why the Video Game Industry has a Responsibility to Empower People with Marginalized and Minority Backgrounds
- Analysis of how storytelling and engaging gaming experiences push the bounds of innovation in the video game industry

"You are a despicable whore." (2015) "I hope you enjoy your last moments alive on this earth. You did nothing worthwhile with your life." (2014) "Better question: Why are you such a whiny bitch? Can't play around on an even playing ground?" (2014) "If you have any kids, they're going to die too. I don't give a fuck. They'll grow up to be feminists anyway." (2014) "Utah State Speech (Cancelled) after mass shooting threat" (October 2014). "Your mutilated corpse will be on the front page of Jezebel tomorrow and there isn't jack shit you can do about it." (2014) "I'm outside your house with a gun." (2014) "If gamer is a race, then it's time for another holocaust." (2014)

Imagine waking up to any of these Tweets or News Headlines from CNN, the Washington Post, and the New York Times, among other media outlets. Your life, which was once private, is now public for the whole world to see in the most terrifying ways. Now everything about yourself, your email, address, and personal information are subject to the whims of people that you don't even know, and they want you to suffer for crimes that you may or may not have committed (point of fact: you are **innocent** of those alleged charges). This is what Zoe Quinn and Brianna Wu, two female independent game developers and Anita Sarkeesian faced over the span of many months in 2014 and 2015. #Gamergate was meant to be a crusade against unethical video game journalism, but it quickly spiraled into a media frenzy that transcended gamers and video game culture.

Sexism is but one of the issues the video game industry has grappled with and still struggles with to this day. Sexism, racial bias, and violence in video games are what define how many non-gamers view the video game industry. As a result, these issues have established the video game industry as not only an industry filled with creativity and innovation, but also as one filled with serious systemic issues that must be solved. It is paramount to understand why sexism, racism, and violence are relevant to the video game industry and its future, most especially in terms of working in the industry and the gaming culture in general. The responsibility of who can solve the problem falls on everyone to promote a con- structive work culture and a positive image for gaming, but independent gaming can and should play a unique role in this process. These not merely problem for the video game industry and independent game developers, they are also areas of opportunity to create new, diverse, and engaging gaming experiences.

The video game industry has been affected by sexism, racism, and violence, but violence in gaming has received the most scrutiny from the outside world. Many non-gamers, who do not know much about the industry or video games in any defined capacity, when they think of video games, think that they engender violent behavior in people who play them. This is a perspective that has persisted almost as long as video games have been around. Because violent video games have received a tremendous amount of publicity, there have been attempts to pass laws regulating the sale of video games. The most notable of which is the 2005 California State Law AB 1179. This law, as innocuous as it might seem, banned the sale of violent video games to anyone under the age of 18 without parent supervision and required labeling that went beyond the existing ESRB rating system label on the package of a video game. The controversial law was challenged on multiple occasions, and it ultimately went before United States Supreme Court in 2010-2011. In Brown v. Entertainment Merchants Association (EMA), the United States Supreme Court in a landmark 7-2 decision, upheld the rulings of the lower courts and declared that the law was unconstitutional because video games were protected under the First Amendment, similarly to other forms of media.

A number of studies have been conducted that allegedly prove a causal connection between violence and video games, but the validity of the studies' findings have been questioned for their supposedly flawed research design. Whenever a shooting takes place in the United States, people against gun control often blame video games as the cause for the shooting. As most recently as the Sandy Hook shooting in 2012, a terrible tragedy, people pointed to how the shooter played violent video games. In fact, the data suggesting a causal link between video games and violent behavior is inconclusive, at best. That has not stopped the media from sensationalizing *Grand Theft Auto* as a video game that engenders violence, a game, which many decry as the embodiment of debauchery and mayhem.

Richard Garriott described the issue of video games as it relates to violent behaviors best:

> "There are three possible conditions – chance is that some people randomly will be some gamers who also are randomly murderers. There's correlation, which means that people that like to murder people probably also like to simulate murdering people. And then there is causality, which would be if playing a game of shooting people causes you to want to go out and shoot people. So, it's really important to know which one of those things it is. Is it something that causes it? Is it something that is correlated? Or is it chance? … One of the most interesting places I've

heard this come up was actually in Korea with our former partners over at NC Soft. The game Lineage was so popular that 1 out of every 10 people in the country plays it. … And yet, what happened one time in Korea, there were a couple of gangs that ended up committing some gang violence, that these gang members also happened to be players of Lineage and they would bad mouth each other in the game and then they would go out in the streets and bang on each other, somebody killed somebody. A lot of people were screaming at the time, saying look at this game Lineage, it is causing people to fight each other in the game and then they go out into the streets and then really finish each other off for real. And it's another one of those cases, where you need to immediately step back and say, "Guys, one out of ten people in the country are playing it. One out of every ten-gang members are playing it. One out of every ten in the opposite gang members are playing it. If these gang members like to yell at each other on the streets, they are going to yell at each other on the virtual streets too. The real problem is that they are gang members."

Regardless of whether or not video games cause violence, there has been a long-standing perception among non-gaming circles that the video game industry is dominated by violent games, such as *Grand Theft Auto* and *Call of Duty*. *Grand Theft Auto* and *Call of Duty* are icons of the video game industry, in that they have broken a litany of sales records, above the $1 Billion and $2 Billion sales marks, but they do not represent the majority of games getting made today.

Parallel to the success of violent video games are sports video games, most notably *FIFA* and *Madden NFL*. To quantify this, both of these gaming franchises have sold over 100 million copies, and *Madden NFL* is considered a $4 Billion franchise in of itself. Moreover, of all the video games rated by the Entertainment Software Rating Board (ESRB), the video game ratings system in the United States, in 2014: M-rated (Mature 17+) games, of which *Call of Duty* and *Grand Theft Auto* are included, made up 14% of video games, whereas 41% of games were rated "E for Everyone." This fact might seem shocking, but to any gamer it is common sense, because from a business perspective, the higher the rating (Teen and Mature 17+), the less likely people will be able to play the game. This logic falls in line with why a number of Hollywood movies are rated PG-13 as opposed to being rated R: sales numbers and revenues matter, because video games are not just entertainment or an art, they are also a business. Therefore, although there are a number of violent video games in the market, less violent or non-violent games such as *FIFA*, *Madden*, among many others should not be marginalized.

What is important to understand and recognize is that there are a number of critically acclaimed and commercially successful *independent* video games that break this normative perception of violence being paramount. Any gamer can point to the narrative, artistic, and gameplay innovations of any of the following games which won Independent Game of the Year at the (Spike Video) Game Awards in their respective years: *Flower* (2009), *Limbo* (2010), *Minecraft* (2011), *Journey* (2012), *Gone Home* (2013), *Shovel Knight* (2014), *Rocket League* (2015), and *Inside* (2016).

Most notably, in 2016, *Inside*, an indie game made by the independent Developer Playdead, which is considered the spiritual successor to *Limbo* was nominated for Game of the Year alongside Overwatch by Blizzard Entertainment, *Uncharted 4: A Thief's End* by Naughty Dog, among other games. The violence present in any of these games is cartoonish at best, but largely non-existent. *Flower* and *Journey*, which were both made by Thatgamecompany and published by Sony, don't include any violence and are hailed as visionary for their artistic design. Some people have questioned whether or not *Gone Home* should even be classified as a game because of how it feels more like art than a *true* game. The main point being, video games, especially independent video games, have found a niche in games that lack the "traditional" violence found in their more sensationalized AAA-counterparts.

It is telling that independent games, not only the ones mentioned, do not rely on violence in order to make for compelling experiences. That is arguably what gaming fundamentally is, an experience to be enjoyed and communally driven – and independent game developers and indie games illustrate this. In talking about the power of online gaming, Richard Garriott, the creator of Ultima, said:

> "What online games do in particular do, they let people of like-minded interest find each other without regard to their geographic disparity and I think that helps re-bond society globally, much less locally back together in ways that we have kind of lost for the last dozens of years through urbanization."

Indie gaming, much like online games, accomplish this same result because they bring people together.

Independent video games also have a stake on the issue of sexism, which is an issue that has torn parts of the video game community apart. Going back to the beginning of this chapter, Zoe Quinn and Brianna Wu were two independent game developers who experienced a level of vitriol that speaks to this issue of sexism in gaming. Notwithstanding the fact that the story of Gamergate is centered on two female game developers, they are independent game developers. According to a 2014 International Game Developer Association (IGDA) study:

- Females represent 22% of in the video game industry workforce
- Men represent 76% of the industry

Moreover, according to the same research, that statistic is up from 11.5% in 2009, so female representation in the industry is on the rise.

The gender imbalance in men to women in the video game industry workforce, makes it all the more recognizable why two female independent game developers faced the brunt of the hostility. Because the video game industry demographics lacks equity, the demographics lend themselves to problematic behavior in the workforce as well as in gaming culture. Female representation is on the rise in gaming, which is why many view Gamergate as a visceral reaction to the change in gaming demographics. It makes logical sense that two female game developers were attacked. But these developers were not just any developers, they are independent, who are the least protected in the video game industry, because they lack the backing of an established company. Therefore, Zoe Quinn and Brianna Wu made for perfect scapegoats for pro-Gamergate supporters, because there was no serious line of defense to prevent them from encountering such hatred on the scale that they did.

Taking a step back, the supposed original intent behind Gamergate was to promote video game journalism ethics.

Zoe Quinn, according to a former boyfriend, "entered into a relationship with a Kotaku journalist, Nathan Grayson" who then gave Zoe Quinn favorable coverage in a piece on her game *Depression Quest*, which was released in 2013. *Depression Quest*, a game that examined Zoe Quinn's own personal experiences with depression, received critical praise for both how it portrayed depression and maintained a level of educational value. The striking thing about *Depression Quest*, according to some, was that Nathan Grayson, who was romantically involved with Zoe Quinn, had written a favorable review of the game. When this scandal was revealed, many immediately became angered at the atrocity that was committed against video game journalism and she started to receive death and rape threats. Aside from the fact that if blame were to be assigned it would need to be distributed on both parties, because Nathan Grayson "actually" performed the corrupt deed in writing a favorable review, none of what people believed about the lack of journalism ethics was true. The "positive review" from the journalist never happened. It was all a witch-hunt that ended up having severe negative impacts on the lives of two female independent game developers.

Zoe Quinn, in writing about her experiences with Gamergate said, "I could have been anybody, all it took was one ex-boy-friend." If Zoe Quinn is right, the spark for Gamergate and the hatred directed towards her and everyone else involved could have applied to anyone else. Brianna Wu suffered collateral damage in that she found her personal information released online because she committed the crime of criticizing Gamergate supporters. Therefore, it is imperative to understand how the video game industry operates and gaming culture manifests itself in response to the issues of gender bias and sexism. Gamergate, gender representation in video games (e.g., hyper- sexualization for female characters, hyper-masculinization for male characters), and the workforce gender breakdown are but a few of the examples people point to when they talk about how gender is a significant, far-reaching issue in the video game industry that needs to be addressed.

Overlay onto this whole picture the statistic that, according to Entertainment Software Association's (ESA) 2014 "State of the Industry Report":

- 48% of all gamers are female – there are more women who game than males 10-25 years old.

These stats underscore the need to find an answer to the issue of gender and video games. One reason for the lack of gender parity in the video game industry might be relatively simple: women have not had as much access to STEM education fields, and the cultural norms were not such that women could have a presence in gaming. Robin Hunicke, a female game developer, was the producer on the both *Flower* and *Journey*. As an advocate for women in the video game industry,

Robin Hunicke, in a 2010 interview with Gamasutra made the following observations:

> "10 years ago, it wouldn't be common for a young woman or a foreign student to be able to express their interests in gaming through a degree program, or even a class. Now that trail has been blazed, and the opportunity is there for a lot of people. Lots of programs have started as one or two classes, and now they're in full enrollment, they're looking for professors. I get tons of e-mails from people looking to hire professors. We've been able to broaden the scope of our recruiting efforts as an industry by exposing more people to the wonder that is video game production. It's not easy work but it's fascinating work, and it's challenging. No two days are alike, and who wouldn't want to work in that industry. We kept it a secret for a while but now the secret is out. Hopefully that means we'll get more diverse people in the work force … more diverse games."

Gender has always been an issue that the video game industry has faced, and in 2013-2014 with the Rise and Fall of Gamergate, the problem was drawn to the forefront. The ongoing "Violence Issue" in games has fueled non-gamers negative perceptions. Moreover, the fact that a strong number of Gamergate supporters sent death and rape threats in addition to the Tweets that Zoe Quinn, Brianna Wu, and Anita Sarkeesian did not help the perception of gaming to the outside world. But at the same time, gender in gaming is constantly evolving. More women are getting into games development and are shaping the workforce, and in time it will hopefully become a non-issue or at least diminished issue.

Karla Zimonja, a female independent game developer, was the co-creator, co-writer, and artist for the critically awarded game *Gone Home*, in 2013. It is important to note that *Gone Home* had a female protagonist. That does not make what happened with Gamergate or any other manifestations of misogyny women face in regards to gaming any less wrong, but this shift highlights that the times are a changing. Independent game development is both symbolic of, and acted as a catalyst for, the change.

The third key issue in the video game industry is race. As a bourgeoning issue in the industry, race has the potential to become the next "Violence Issue" or "Gamergate" in gaming. According to a 2005 IGDA study:

- 7.5% of game developers were Asian
- 2.5% of developers were Hispanic
- A mere 2% of developers were African-American

Rich Taylor, Senior Vice President of Communications and Industry affairs at the Entertainment Software Association (ESA), the trade association for the video game industry, said in 2013:

> "This is something that I am personally passionate about. I am African-American and I see that there is room for greater representation not just in gaming but the entertainment industry as a whole. I came from the motion picture industry and there was a similar landscape there."

The problem Rich Taylor and many others have with a lack of racial diversity in the video game industry (similarly to gender) is not that they want diversity for the sake of diversity, but rather having people from a variety of different backgrounds allows for a greater level of diversity of thought. This harkens back to the fact that the video game industry is at the intersection of technology and entertainment. From a business perspective, it is important to keep in mind that diversity of thought enhances the potential for creative thinking that can produce entertainment that is appealing to more people, which means better sales numbers.

The lack of racial diversity in the industry workforce also explains the lack of racially diverse video game characters that exist and the racial stereotypes that persist as a result. In 2016, *Mafia III*, a AAA-game that received positive reviews as the third entry into the *Mafia* franchise, had an African-American leading character. *Mafia* III, which was set in 1968, at the height of racial tensions and the Civil War in the United

States had Lincoln Clay, a Vietnam War veteran returning to a fictionalized "New Orleans," known as New Bordeaux. The game told the story of his rise to prominence as the leader of the *Mafia* in New Bordeaux and how he created the crime syndicate from the ground up. On its face, Lincoln Clay's story is a true American-crime drama story, but looking a little bit deeper, Lincoln Clay is but one of only a handful of black leading characters in video games. There are examples of Lee Everett from Telltale's *The Walking Dead* (2012) or Alyx Vance from *Half-Life 2* (2004), but by and large they are the token examples of racial diversity in video games protagonists and leading characters.

Outside of the concerns that the majority of black and racially diverse characters are typecast or stereotyped and made to be antagonists or comic relief, video game representation in terms of race has not received as much attention as gender has. As it was for women in gaming, problems such as financial barriers, lack of training, and almost no opportunity are considered leading factors among developers as to why there is a lack of racial diversity in gaming. With time and the reduction of these barriers, race will reduce the problem.

There is a website called "blackgamedevs.com" that has a list of Black Game Developers. The website's tagline is, "Here they are. Hire them. Buy their stuff."

The purpose of the website is to promote the black identity in gaming, thus the social media handles for these developers is linked to the people listed. Black Game Developers specifically showcases black independent game developers. The idea behind the website is that through promoting developers in a grassroots way, actionable change can occur within the video game industry. Time will tell if efforts such as this website, and the demographic and socioeconomic shifts taking place within the United States and other parts of the world will result in any difference in the video game industry. But this issue far extends beyond white and black; race in gaming is relevant for everyone. Similarly, to gender and violence, independent gaming is at the forefront in tackling these matters.

In talking about the importance of diversity and mentorship in the video game industry, Jennifer Bullard, Director of Program Management at Querium, said:

> "I focused on helping people that are disadvantaged with whatever information or knowledge that I have. Whether it was disadvantaged children that don't have access to college educated adults. I have also done some coaching and mentoring for those coming into the industry, to encourage women and minorities to enter because diversity definitely helps projects. The best video games are when the team has been culturally diverse. A large part of it was just passing along my good fortune."

Supporters of diversity in the workplace in the video game industry, whether it be in terms of gender identity, race, sexual orientation, or any other factor, believe that mentorship as Jennifer talks about is the hallmark of what diversity is all about and the business value that diversity can bring to game development. Diversity plays a role in developing better games because it brings new and different perspectives to the table that allows for a more informed discussion on games development. Diversity and mentorship are important in these ways because, just as an effective team needs to have competent writers, game designers, and artists, the closer a team can get to having a myriad of voices on the project the better the team culture will be. In work cultures that lack strong leadership many default to believing that homogeneous teams work better. It takes a true leader to realize that marshaling the talents of a diverse team will more often result in a superior outcome. This more enlightened approach allows the opportunity for a greater offering of more diverse games in a variety of genres, which increases sales and is something that independent developers excel at already.

Independent game developers have the distinct opportunity to lead and be the catalyst for needed change with regard to issues of violence, gender bias, and racial bias in the video game industry. Said differently, a viable way to break into the industry is to recognize the shortcomings of what exists and offer disruptive solutions to these pressing concerns. In a number of ways, through their innovations in the games that are getting made, who is making the games and how decisions get made in game development, independent developers can be at the forefront of these issues. In large part, independent developers are creating positive change in the video game industry because they are people pursuing their passion for making games. Of note, Independent developers are not immune to these issues, because the developer community is still majority male and majority white, and there is a lack of equity and parity in the indie space on these issues, but strides are being made. These strides not only change the face of the video game industry, they also shine a light on and elevate the quality of the discourse when it comes to these particular video game industry issues.

KEY INSIGHTS AND TAKEAWAY LESSONS

- The video game industry is controversial regarding the issues of gender bias, racial bias, and violent content, which are largely criticisms of AAA games
  - Independent developers are known to make games that provide different and nuanced perspectives on these issues
  - As an indie developer, these are potential opportunity areas to address these issues when making a game
- White males dominate AAA gaming, and a shift needs to happen.

- People from diverse backgrounds and faiths are already making a number of indie games, but this can be pushed even further.
- Considering 48% of all gamers are female, there is an opportunity to cater to different audiences by making engaging games that are not "stereotypical" or "gender biased" in both character portrayal and gaming experience.

ADDITIONAL INDUSTRY VETERAN PERSPECTIVE:

"An enduring problem with any business of finding great people. You can have the most genius idea in the world but if you don't have a team to execute that idea it isn't worth anything."

— PETER MOLYNEUX (FOUNDER, LIONHEAD STUDIOS AND 22CANS)

"My approach to things and ideas starts from curiosity. I find it important to challenge general thinking and do something against it. For me thinking out of the box is about doing smaller innovations or extreme opposites of something. That said, I don't think thinking outside of the box actually narrows our thinking. Even if the point is to think innovatively. ... Instead of doing things opposite or starting from one idea, my approach to 'new' is different. For me it is more about "what if" and

using various methods to challenge the ideas and to strive for something potentially very far from 'the box'."

— SONJA ÄNGESLEVÄ (MENTOR, GAMEFOUNDERS)

PART 2

FINDING
A VOICE

CHAPTER 4

INDEPENDENT GAME DEVELOPERS THRIVING IN GAMING

———

"I'm going to run my own studio and the main reason is I want to build my own games."

— MARK COOKE (FOUNDER AND CEO, SHINY SHOE)

CHAPTER FOCUS:

- Documenting the Experiences of Independent Game Developers
- Examination of Different Paths and Reasons People had for "going indie"

- Conversation on the Responsibility (and Ownership of One's Future) one takes on in "going indie"
- Develop a perspective of "success" in Indie Gaming

Dan Brady accomplished the impossible. When he was CEO of Blue Castle Games, Dan Brady pushed the envelope of innovation when working on *Dead Rising 2*, an entry in a major AAA Video Game Franchise. He did this because Blue Castle was an underdog. Blue Castle Games was a relatively small company that was given the opportunity, with *Dead Rising 2*, to punch above their weight class and make a game that could potentially be played by millions of people. But before Blue Castle was able to secure its identity as the creator of future *Dead Rising* Games, they had to start somewhere.

Founded in 2005, in Burnaby, British Columbia, Canada Blue Castle had 12 employees. By 2007, with only 12 employees, they were known as the studio behind *The Bigs*, a major baseball video game. *The Bigs* was a multi-platform game on the Xbox 360, PlayStation 3, PlayStation 2, the PlayStation Portable, and the Wii. Blue Castle got the game published by 2K Sports, a major player in the sports game space. For the work that they did, in February 2008, Blue Castle was named the Best New Video Game Company at the 2008 Elan Awards. But when Blue Castle Games was awarded the contract to make the sequel to the cult classic hit, *Dead Rising*, everyone thought that Blue Castle Games would fail. The company had to quickly grow to 170 people, and take on one of their biggest projects — only their 2nd major project at the time.

When Blue Castle Games was signed on to make *Dead Rising 2*, everyone thought that they would fail. Dan Brady on the challenges that Blue Castle faced said:

> "We had an awful challenge, an awful large challenge, actually trying to convince everyone in the industry that we had the knowledge and the skill-set to actually make something like *Dead Rising*, given that Blue Castle had only really published The Bigs before that."

Blue Castle Games, when it came down to it, was a yet untested company. They had made a successful arcade sports title, but nothing on the caliber of what a traditional AAA-game required.

But somehow Blue Castle succeeded. Against all the odds and in the face of all of the doubt, they did what nobody thought they could. Dan Brady said:

> "When we made *Dead Rising 2*, you could call it a sequel, but we made the entire development engine from scratch. We didn't use any of the code, and very few of the art assets, from the first game."

As a young up-start company, Blue Castle Games went from being a small company to making one of the Largest AAA titles of 2010 (over 2.2 million copies sold worldwide).

Blue Castle Games was able to accomplish all of this because the developers at the studio saw the video game that they had to develop, reflected on their own experiences and expertise, and found how they could relate the two to one another. Many of the people at Blue Castle had worked on Fighting Games in the past. The *Dead Rising* series mechanically operated very much like a wrestling/fighting game.

As a result of Blue Castle's success with *Dead Rising 2*, Capcom, a company most famously known for the Street Fighter franchise and the Resident Evil series, acquired the development studio. Moreover, since *Dead Rising 2*, Blue Castle Games, now Capcom Vancouver, has gone on to make every *Dead Rising* entry to date, with the most recent release of *Dead Rising 4* in 2016.

Although Dan Brady's story highlights video game development in the AAA-ecosystem, his story nevertheless lends itself to the independent developer experience. Much like many independent game developers, Dan Brady accomplished what he did with limited resources, compacted and demanding project timelines, an ambitious vision for the game, and a lack of credibility from the outside world's perspective.

Independent game developers in the industry, much like their corporate counterparts, make video games because it is something they are passionate about. The key difference being, unlike a AAA-developer, who, when they are limited by a set of constraints, at the very least have corporate backing from a parent company or a publisher to ensure that they get the game out the door and have relative paycheck security in the process. Independent game developers, therefore in a number of ways are very unique in the pursuit of their craft, and deserve their stories to be told.

When gamers talk about indie gaming, they often times are able point to their favorite indie game, but there is not a guarantee that they will always know the individual developer or small team of developers behind the project. But even if said gamer knows who the independent developer is, one of the most notable examples being Markus "Notch" Persson (Creator of *Minecraft*), even fewer know how or why that person became an independent game developer. For every independent game developer, there is a story of imagination and creativity, a desire to solve problems, and a passion for what they do.

For every independent developer, there is a unique and fascinating story that can be told. Some independent game developers have similar stories and reasoning as to why they ended up where they did. But one thing is clear, in becoming independent game developers each person found that they were capable of innovating in the video game industry in their own way. Therefore, it is important to listen to and understand their stories if one is to truly appreciate the value that they bring to the video game industry as pioneering figures. In this chapter, you will read about their stories and learn more about their different paths to becoming independent game developers and why they felt an imperative to pursue their path.

THE STORY OF MARK COOKE, CEO (SHINY SHOE)

Mark Cooke founded Shiny Shoe, an independent game development studio based in San Francisco, California, in 2011. Shiny Shoe is a company that splits its time between building original games and consulting with clients such as Double Fine Productions, Telltale, and WB Games. Mark Cooke, like many independent game developers, also had a career in the video game industry before going independent. In talking about his decision to go indie, Mark conveyed what most indie developers might share as their first reason for going independent, "I'm going to run my own studio and the main reason is I want to build my own games." But he went on to say that he was moved by his first taste of the business side of games:

"When you're running a studio, especially if you grow,

there's a whole list of other business tasks that come along with that (creating and running your own studio). ... I wasn't getting enough exposure as I wanted so by starting your own company you're going to get exposed to everything very quickly."

For Mark Cooke, it was not solely his passion for making video games that drove his decision to become an independent developer, but also his desire to learn more about business. More generally, the desire to know more about the business of games, Mark explained, came from his desire to problem solve and learn new ideas.

Shiny Shoe, as an independent developer, creates both its own indie games as well as works on consulting projects with larger, more established companies. Mark Cooke, when speaking on Shiny Shoe's indie games, calls them "original games." This is worth noting because it speaks to a mentality within games development, that either a game is original or it is not original. In viewing indie games as original games, there is a new level of meaning endowed in what it means to be an independent game developer. As an independent developer making an original game, you are forging your own path as a content creator and visionary, as opposed to simply making a game as an independent developer. As a studio, Shiny Shoe worked in tandem with Double Fine Productions on *Grim Fandango*, a remastered version of the LucasArts classic title that was released in 2015. This different approach for a video game company is interestingly enough how a number of independent studios are able to survive and thrive in the industry, because consulting work allows for additional streams of income outside of the traditional route of making your own games.

One of the things that Mark attributes to his career and an independent game developer is his desire to work on the best and most challenging project. Mark said that for him it is important to:

> "Try to work on the best things all the time – it is a real challenge and it's almost unknowable. You can never know exactly what the best thing is but you use your judgment and experience to *try* and *make* good decisions."

Mark is right, going out of your comfort zone is important, and as an independent developer he recognizes that his interest to learn more about the business of games came directly from this philosophy.

THE STORY OF SEAN VANAMAN, CO-FOUNDER (CAMPO SANTO)

Sean Vanaman is a game designer and writer, and he previously worked for Telltale Games and Walt Disney Company. Sean Vanaman made a name for himself while he was at Telltale

Games, an American independent game developer and publisher founded June 2004. While at Telltale Games, Sean was the project lead on *Poker Night at the Inventory* (2010) and *The Walking Dead* (2012). In addition to being the project lead, Sean was also the lead writer for Telltale's *The Walking Dead*. *The Walking Dead*, an episodic interactive drama and graphic adventure video game, a game based on the TV-series, has won over 80 Game of the Year Awards and other accolades since its initial release in 2012; it won Game of the Year in 2012 at the Video Game Awards. Clearly, Sean had played in the big leagues and had wildly succeeded.

But Sean Vanaman left Telltale Games to co-found Campo Santo, a San Francisco based independent video game development studio, in 2013; the company currently has 11 employees. Sean Vanaman on his decision to leave Telltale and co-found Campo Santo, wrote in one of Campo Santo's first blog posts:

> "Deciding to found and then actually create a video game studio has felt like a mix of buying a winning lottery ticket and taking a brushed detour that results in a near mess with the pedestrian."

He goes on to say:

> "Some of us want to tell stories, some of us want to build

systems and some of us want to create beautiful looking worlds." He writes, *"But we all want to make something."*

Sean's reason for leaving his successful career at Telltale Games and co-found an independent studio harkens back to his desire, along with his colleagues, to "make something." Considering Sean is a writer, an especially creative role within the video game industry, which is largely creative and entertainment driven, this makes logical sense. But what is truly striking about Sean's passion for making games and pursuing the path of an independent games development is that Sean is leveraging his expertise and talents as a writer and experience in the industry. Prior to leaving and co-founding Campo Santo, he worked at Telltale Games, a developer and publisher that found a niche in acquiring rights to franchising games within larger brands (*The Walking Dead*, *Borderlands*, *Game of Thrones*, *Minecraft* and many more).

Sean was a writer for Campo Santo's first game *Firewatch*, which was released in 2016. *Firewatch*, a first-person mystery adventure game, focuses on a national forest fire lookout named, Henry. It was set in 1989, after a major fire happened in Yellow Stone in 1988. *Firewatch* went on to be nominated for a number of Joystick Awards and Video Game Awards, and the game won the award for Best 3D Visual Experience at the Unity Awards in 2016 and Best Indie Game at the 2016 Golden Joystick Awards. *Firewatch* was hailed by critics for its engaging narrative and sense of realism, despite the stylized level design and art design for the game. Further, Campo Santo and Good Universe, an indie film production company, are signed on to make a *Firewatch* film. Most of all, *Firewatch* as of the end of 2016, has sold over one million copies. These data points highlight what is within the realm of possibility when an independent game developer succeeds.

By all accounts, the critical and commercial triumph Campo Santo experienced with *Firewatch* is an anomaly in the indie gaming space. Not every independent game by design can accomplish this by design. In a lot of ways, though, Sean's career path, leaving a budding career at Telltale, to co-found an independent studio is representative of a good number of independent developers. He proves the power of first learning the craft at a major developer and then going out to combine those experiences with a passion to make something on one's own. There are a solid number of independent game developers who leave their corporate or more established careers in the industry to "*go indie*." One of the main reasons behind why people leave and "go indie" is because they want to "make something."

THE STORY OF BRANDON BECK & MARC MERRILL, CO-FOUNDERS (*RIOT GAMES*)

Brandon Beck and Marc Merrill are the Co-founders of Riot

Games, a company founded in 2006. Brandon Beck and Marc Merrill have a non-traditional story relative to other video game developers in the industry. Unlike an average video game developer, Brandon Beck and Marc Merrill do not have degrees in computer science, mathematics, or engineering. Brandon left his job at Bain & Company as a Management Consultant, and Marc left his job at Advantar Communication as a Corporate Marketing Executive when they co-founded Riot Games.

Due to the fact that Brandon and Marc have backgrounds that are different than most independent game developers, Riot Games is not your average video game company. Riot Games is a video game developer, publisher, and eSports Tournament organizer based out of Los Angeles, California.

When Riot Games was originally founded, the studio was an independent developer, but since 2011 they are longer independent. With *League of Legends*, which brought on the second coming of and the ultimate rise of eSports, Riot Games quickly became a breakout video game company that rivaled many AAA-developers. With all these things in mind, Riot Games, although it is a video game company, has positioned itself as a savvy business player in the context of eSports and video game monetization. *League of Legends* operates on a free-to-play business model, but through sponsors, partnerships, competitive gaming, micro-transactions, and other revenue streams, Riot Games created a successful business.

Through the popularity of *League of Legends*, eSports has taken video game culture and the media by storm. Mark Cuban, successful entrepreneur and owner of the Dallas Mavericks, invested in 2015 in a gaming startup related to betting on eSports games (Unikrn). Mark Cuban has often joked that he thinks investing in an eSports team would be highly lucrative, but went on the record in 2016 saying that he would not buy a team just yet because the eSports market was too volatile. Mark Cuban recognized that although eSports gaming is on the rise, teams are being bought and sold quickly, player burnout is a major concern, and general investment in a team in the short term might potentially be more than its worth. None of these things have stopped Riot Games from being a successful promoter of eSports or a competitive business.

In 2011 Tencent Holdings Company, a Chinese investment holding company with interests in media, entertainment, Internet, and mobile phone services, bought a majority stake in Riot Games. As of 2015, Tencent Holdings owns Riot Games in its entirety. Outside investment from foreign investors and venture capital are meaningful ways that have helped elevate Riot Games to another level, whether or not it becomes a trend in the video game industry as a whole is up to independent developers and how they want to receive funding for their games.

But even as a subsidiary of a major holding company, Riot Games has tried to maintain its independent roots despite the fact that it no longer is an independent games company. One of the things Riot Games strives towards is to be the *"most player focused"* game company in the world. At the 2015 D.I.C.E. Summit Marc talked about the core values that he and Brandon have developed throughout their lives and how it influenced how the early days of Riot Games. According to Marc, one of the things that matters most in terms of games development is not technology, intellectual property, game design, but rather people. Marc elaborated in this D.I.C.E. Summit talk that creating great teams will make or break a company. Logically, this passes a reasonability test, because the people and the culture that surrounds them ultimately defines the quality of the game getting made. More than that, though, Riot Games has a number of the original developers who made *Defense of the Ancients* (DOTA), which *League of Legends* is primarily based on. This fact, along with the culture of gaming that Riot Games has tried to engender, where passion matters, Riot Games had and still has a recipe for success. When it comes to thinking outside of the box, Riot Games has a philosophy that the way to solve any problem is to bring smart, talented people from a multitude of diverse backgrounds together, motivate them around a common mission, and allow them to think and share creatively with each other.

Brandon and Marc, when they founded Riot Games, saw a problem in the video game industry, that not all shareholders, boardroom members, gamers, and companies have people as their priority. Marc went on in his D.I.C.E. Summit talk to say that he believes that is what will hold the video game industry back from achieving its full potential. In a way, that problem recognition paired with a passion for video games is what drove Riot Games to be the effective developer that it is. As a result of Brandon and Marc's unorthodox talent backgrounds, they bring a different, yet dynamic perspective to the video game industry.

If a gamer were to be asked about *League of Legends* and what they knew about the game, they would point to how *League of Legends* has spawned some of the largest eSports Tournaments of all time. Although Brandon and Marc are technically not independent game developers, because *League of Legends* is no longer an indie game, they still exemplify a passion for gaming that exists in independent game developers.

THE STORY OF MICHAEL TURNER, CEO AND FOUNDER (WE THE PLAYERS)

Michael Turner created a start-up called We the Players. We the Players, in Michael's words was, "a proposal-based feedback platform for game developers." The idea behind it is that when developers make changes to a game in order to create a sense of balance, there is not usually feedback between the developers and the community surrounding the given game. For a game, such as *Call of Duty*, if Infinity Ward, Treyarch, or Sledgehammer Games, depending on how made the most recent *Call of Duty* in that year, wanted to make a change, We the Players would allow the *Call of Duty* gaming community to voice their opinions. In the most ideal of circumstances, it would create communication and trust between developers and gamers. Michael had left his job at Delta Air Lines to create the company. Michael Turner's venture lasted from 2013-2016, and, ultimately, he became a project engineer at AIS-International, Ltd, and re-entered the air travel agency.

In speaking about why he wanted to create We the Players, Michael said:

> **That's really a desire to create something unique.** I've worked for a big company before, in the airline industry. There's nothing wrong working for a big company, it's just that it is not exactly breeding grounds for creativity. So, for my desire to create something new, I had this gaming idea, and I wanted to see if I could create something from scratch … There's really something about creating something that wasn't there before, and *having an impact on people* that is very attractive to me."

As it was the case many independent game developers, Michael

Turner left a corporate career in the attempt to create a company in the video game industry focused on a key pressure point between gamers and game developers. Although Michael Turner was not successful, which is common in the video game industry, he nevertheless entered the video game industry based on his passion for video games and solving problems.

Michael also spoke about what fascinated him about innovation:

"There can be a lot of people along the way that give you a lot of different reasons why your product, your service won't work and there comes a point where you just have to *reject all the naysayers* and keep moving forward to really create something new. New things and innovative things by definition are untested. And so, it can be very difficult before anything is proven to be sure that something is going to work. There will always be people saying this doesn't exist now for a reason and no one has done it for a reason, it doesn't work. So, you do have to be persistent and go forward with your vision."

This philosophy is very similar to that of Peter Molyneux, the creator of *Fable* as well as the Founder of both Lionhead Studios and more recently 22 Cans. Michael loved that with We The Players he was able to take on new ideas, challenge himself, and experiment in ways that he had not previously done so. Although We The Player was not a video game like what many independent game developers normally make, the idea still holds true that Michael is similar both in spirit and attitude to an independent game developer.

THE STORY OF BRETT DOUVILLE, INDEPENDENT GAME DEVELOPER (*MY DIVORCE*)

Brett Douville is an independent game developer who has previously worked for both LucasArts and Bethesda Softworks. While at LucasArts, Brett Douville was one of the lead developers on *Star Wars Starfighter*, *Star Wars Jedi Starfighter*, and *Star Wars Republic Commando*, which are all games that many gamers hold a great level of nostalgia towards. When Brett Douville worked at Bethesda, two of his more notable projects were *Fallout 3* and *Elder Scrolls V: Skyrim*, which are both games that have won Game of the Year and RPG of the Year.

Brett Douville is a prototypical independent game developer. One of his personal games that he has developed is called *My Divorce*, which is a game that was inspired by Rod Humble's *The Marriage*. *My Divorce* was a game that Brett made in response to when he divorced his wife and the implications that it had not only on his life but also on his children. The purpose of the game was to examine the impact a divorce has on a family. When Brett spoke about what he appreciates about being an independent developer and how he views innovation, he said:

"It's a question of focus and iteration — games are made better by only containing in them what you have time to truly devote yourselves to, and to have time to iterate and polish those things. Innovation sometimes occurs from familiarity with how things have worked and choosing to break some of "*the rules*," but you can only do that if you're familiar with the rules."

Brett Douville, an industry veteran who understands "the rules," felt that when it comes to innovation, and being a successful independent game developer, experience matters.

More pointedly, when talking about where he believes innovation in the video game industry most exists, Brett replied:

"The other place where we're seeing a lot of innovation is in the indie space, of course, though those games are mostly not terribly lucrative (the exceptions get all the publicity) and so it would be a difficult model for bigger games to follow. I think it's still true that innovation happens there as a result of understanding games really deeply and trying to achieve weird new twists as a result. There's also the naturally focusing factor of not having tons of money or time to put into development, so Indies have to say "no" to a thousand things."

As Steve Jobs once said, "innovation is saying no to a thousand things." As an independent developer, Brett echoes this way of thinking to the letter.

Brett has developed his philosophies on game design and the video game industry through his personal passion for video games as well as creating and solving new problems. Brett firmly embodies these two core values like any independent game developer in the video game industry.

THE STORY OF JONATHAN BLOW, INDEPENDENT GAME DEVELOPER (BRAID, 2008)

Jonathan Blow is an independent game developer, both programmer and designer by trade. Jonathan is best known as a creator of *Braid* (2008), a game which game received critical acclaim, and more recently, he worked on the game *The Witness* (2016), which also received critical praise.

Jonathan is perhaps the closest anyone can get to an independent developer and image as the *ideal* independent game developer. The reason for that is because he is a **self-driven** software developer:

> "I don't feel accountable to the world to make things for them. I look out there at the games that are really popular and they're not really usually the games that I'm excited about. It's fine if it's somebody's job to make the biggest

hits, and apparently that job is for Rockstar or Ubisoft or something. ... I'm doing something different."

That is exactly what Jonathan Blow did with *Braid*. When Jonathan first started out in 2005, he self-funded *Braid*, a game with a budget of $200,000. When Jonathan finished the game in late 2008, after working on it for three years, he was $40,000 in debt.

Braid, a platform and puzzle video game, focuses on a protagonist (Tim), who attempts to rescue a princess from a monster, a textbook story out of Mario. But what made the game truly great in the eyes of critics is that the game made masterful use of time manipulation, puzzle solving, level design, and overall narrative. One critic praised the philosophical complexity of the game saying:

> "Jonathan Blow's *Braid* is the sort of ontological labyrinth that Jorge Luis Borges might have made. Embedded in the simple gameplay design are genuinely huge concepts."

Braid, on every account, was a "perfect video game," and the commercial success that followed, many would say, was well deserved. As of 2015, *Braid* had made almost $6 million, which Jonathan used to fund his next game, *The Witness*.

One might think that Jonathan would appreciate the wealth

that *Braid* generated for him, and like most anybody else, would want to indulge in a lavish lifestyle. This could not be further from the truth for Jonathan, when talking about his success, Jonathan has said in interviews:

> "It just drives home how fictional money is. One day I'm looking at my bank account and there's not much money, and the next day there's a large number in there and I'm rich. In both cases, it's a fictional number on the computer screen, and the only reason that I'm rich is because somebody typed a number into my bank account."

Moreover, of the money that he made from *Braid*, Jonathan only spent enough money on himself to get a new car (Tesla Roadster) and a new, spacious condo – Jonathan invested the rest in development on *The Witness*. Moreover, Jonathan has stated:

> "I've never liked money, really. Having a big high score in my bank account is not interesting to me. I have a nice car now, but I don't really own that many objects, and I don't know what else I would spend money on. So, for me, money is just a tool I can use to get things done."

That is what defines Jonathan as an independent game developer. Jonathan wants to make technically challenging games, not in the Blockbuster (*Call of Duty*) technically challenging way, but rather in a cerebral and existential way. Jonathan as a game developer is motivated by his passion, the pursuit of the art of making video games.

Jonathan's *Braid* is a game that represents a turning point in the growth of the independent game development scene. Although not every independent video game developer by design can make a game that is as successful as *Braid*, *Braid* further legitimized independent video games as both an art form and a business. Jonathan exemplifies the innate desire of independent game developers, he does not just want to "make something," he wants to be challenged and challenge others; he wants to push the envelope of video game design. Jonathan's chosen project for this is *The Witness*, because, "I want to make games for people who read Gravity's Rainbow."

Jonathan's story, much like many independent game developers, is about a pursuit based on passion and intellectual curiosity. Some independent game developers are more successful than others, and that is how the video game industry, much like any other industry, operates. But what is truly telling about independent game developers is that they are not tethered by a larger company or shareholders to define to them what they can or cannot do – *they are the makers of their own destiny.*

THE STORY JOSUHE PAGLIERY, CUBA'S FIRST INDEPENDENT GAME DEVELOPER (*SAVIOR*)

Savior, a game made by Josuhe Pagliery, is poised to be the first independent video game created entirely in Cuba; this is an endeavor first started in 2016. Josuhe is the Director, art designer, and screenwriter for *Savior*, and he is working with his colleague Johann, a programmer. *Savior* is a 2D platformer game that makes use of time mechanics and other experimental mechanics. At first glance, if one did not know any better, the game might sound like *Braid*, which was made by Jonathan Blow. But what makes *Savior* a truly unique game is that the game's success will play an integral role in determining whether or not future games will ever be made in Cuba. In talking about some of the challenges Josuhe and his team have faced, in an interview with Polygon he said:

> "It is as if we had to rediscover for ourselves every aspect of developing a game, in addition to an almost obsolete equipment. Things that are completely normal for every other developer, like owning a bank account, starting a company, running a crowdfunding campaign ... constitute great obstacles for us."

These are monumental challenges for Josuhe because he is in Cuba, a country severely crippled by the historical lack of U.S.-Cuban relations. Considering the international implications of living and working in Cuba, Josuhe and Johann are developing *Savior* under the most uncertain of circumstances. There is the possibility that with a change in foreign relations between the two countries, *Savior* might never see the light of day.

In talking about why it is so important that they finish the game and succeed, Josuhe conveyed that he wanted *Savior* as a game, much like the game's narrative, to be a beacon of hope:

> "We want *Savior* to the first example of a successful video game for independent developers in the country, something that might ***give others hope*** and encouragement, and make them think: 'If they could finish *Savior* and succeed in the midst of all these difficulties, then maybe we can do it too.'"

In the context of Cuba, Josuhe is saying that *Savior* has the potential to make indie gaming become a robust ecosystem in the country. More generally, though, Josuhe's sentiment can be applied to what indie gaming represents: a ground-level entry for anyone with a passion for video games and wants to make a career out of making games. Moreover, indie gaming is able to be that beacon of hope, especially in Cuba, because indie gaming is able to exist and thrive in places where AAA gaming cannot. Against all the odds, Josuhe Pagliery has the opportunity of a lifetime to expand the video game industry expand into Cuba through indie gaming.

Dan Brady, as someone with experience solely in the AAA space of gaming, highlights how the thought process of an entrepreneur can make a development studio an unlikely competitor. Mark Cooke highlights how a desire to learn more, much like Ralph Baer, can allow someone to get off the treadmill and find their own path. Sean Vanaman shows that innate desire to "create something" is a truth for the most successful independent game developers. Brandon Beck and Marc Merrill show that even without a traditional engineering or software development background, it is possible to make a name for oneself and leave a lasting mark on video games. Michael Turner and Brett Douville both showcase how it is important to constantly iterate and reinvent old ideas to make them relevant across time. Jonathan Blow is an independent developer who pursued his passion for making games no matter the cost, and used his financial rewards to continue making games. Josuhe Pagliery's journey and his game *Savior* show that regardless of where independent game developers find their start, they have the potential to create of a culture of gaming almost anywhere and in any place.

While they all have different stories in how they entered the video game industry, there is a common thread between all of them: they all love video games. These independent developers have gone on to varying degrees of success, financial stability, and notoriety in the video game industry for the ways in which they embody the innovation of the video game industry, especially in the indie gaming scene. These developers all come from different walks of life, but they have found success and meaning in their own ways, which raises the question as to how they find guidance now as indie developers. The short answer is through their professional and social networks. But there are many paths to success. Therefore, it is an imperative for an independent developer your path and follow it to its furthest, hardest, scariest journey and ultimate destination.

KEY INSIGHTS AND TAKEAWAY LESSONS

- Indie developers have many different backgrounds, but they all have a common set of factors that led them to going indie:
  - Creating Things is important
  - Problem solving is enjoyable
  - Ownership and responsibility in a small team setting is engaging
  - They have a passion for video games
- The vast majority of indie developers who succeed have some degree of video game industry experience – just like in the entrepreneurship world, you can't go out and make it big—it takes practice.
- Valuing people and the dynamics of a team are important in order to be a successful indie developer – be team focused as well as player focused.
- Persistence might not always result in success, but it is important to take the leap of faith if you want to even have a shot.

ADDITIONAL INDUSTRY VETERAN PERSPECTIVE:

"If you're interested in being a designer, I'd recommend that you learn at least the basics of programming as it will help you in your career. If you really don't want to, however, make a mod for another game using their existing design tools."

— MARK COOKE (CEO, SHINY SHOE)

"If you're an artist work on your fundamentals - both 2d and 3d. It's also valuable to understand some of the technical aspects of getting an asset into a game engine. So I recommend trying to not just build art in Photoshop or Maya but also to try to get it into a game. Partner up with a programmer to get art into your awesome version of Pong."

— MARK COOKE (CEO, SHINY SHOE)

"Our approach is to surrounds ourselves with smart, talented people with diverse backgrounds and perspectives. Once you have that team, you then have to allow them to think and share creatively. We want to cultivate a culture in which everyone feels empowered to share and fight for their ideas."

— BLAKE EDWARDS ON RIOT GAMES' PHILOSOPHY
(PLAYER RELATIONS SPECIALIST, RIOT GAMES)

CHAPTER 5

LEVEL-UP: HOW INDEPENDENT DEVELOPERS CAN MAKE A NAME FOR THEMSELVES

———

"If you like video games, you can make your own job, create your own market and just befriend people, get friendly, get the word out there and it will go for you."

— DAVID VOYLES (SENIOR TECHNICAL
EVANGELIST, MICROSOFT)

CHAPTER FOCUS:

- Discussion on Entrepreneurship and How Independent Game Developers are the Entrepreneurs of the Video Game Industry
- What it means to be entrepreneurial in the Video Game Industry
- Assessment of Why Indie-Entrepreneurs Developers can change the Video Game Industry in a meaningful way
- How to Avoid the trap of becoming a "wantrapreneur"

Markus "Notch" Persson, the creator of *Minecraft* wrote in his blog upon leaving Mojang and *Minecraft* after selling the company to Microsoft, "I'm not a CEO. I'm a nerdy computer programmer who likes to have opinions on Twitter." Markus might not be a CEO of a company, but he is not simply "a nerdy computer programmer." Markus is an innovator, a video game icon for the creation of *Minecraft*. Whether or not he personally believes this to be true, his work speaks for itself. His work shows that although he might not be a CEO of a company, he was an entrepreneur who created a start-up company, called Mojang. As an independent developer, Markus developed Mojang's first product, *Minecraft*, a game that redefined the video game industry on a multitude of levels. With the launch of *Minecraft* in the spring of 2009 Markus entered the big leagues of video game entrepreneurs.

Everyone in the video game industry, to some degree, has an entrepreneurial mindset. And independent game developers are some of the most extreme entrepreneurs. This is perhaps one of the unrecognized truths about the video game industry. As a $100+ Billion industry, video games have been praised for their technological innovations, most recently in regards to virtual reality and its applicability beyond entertainment in areas such as education and organizational development. Many people love video games especially in regards to how they push the envelope of storytelling and entertainment value as a medium. A common praise of video game is that they can be seen as an art form. According to Statista, an online statistics platform:

- People spend a daily average of 23.2 minutes per capita playing video games (2014 Data)
- Households, on average, spend $60.92 on video games every year (2013 Data).

By multiple measures, people have a deep appreciation and make time for video games. But what is not often talked about in any genuine capacity is the entrepreneurship of the video game industry and how lessons learned from this industry could be applied to elevate other industry.

At the AAA-gaming level, there is a growing desire among companies to be more entrepreneurial. With EA Originals and other similar initiatives among major companies, there is a subtle, yet noticeable shift in the industry towards creating a more entrepreneurial culture. When Ralph Baer created the

Magnavox Odyssey and in the early days of the video game industry, entrepreneurial tendencies manifested themselves. Eric Koester, Founder & Chief Instigator at Kingmaker Labs and serial entrepreneur, in a short video with FounderFilms, asserted, "You don't necessarily have to be an entrepreneur in order to be entrepreneurial." He went on to say, "*Being entrepreneurial is a state of mind*, it is not something that you do."

Matt Hansen, COO at Double Fine Productions, does not believe that he is an entrepreneur, which is understandable from a traditional thinking standpoint given he has not started his own company or pursued some sort of endeavor in a capacity where he took on risk to a degree than an entrepreneur would. But Matt does consider himself to be entrepreneurial at heart.

Matt Hansen left Telltale Games for Double Fine Productions because he was intrigued by Double Fine's decision to shift to smaller projects. By working on smaller projects, the employees at Double Fine are able to work on even smaller teams and take on greater ownership and responsibility with any given project. This is perhaps as close as someone might be able to find in the video game industry where a video game developer at a AA or AAA games company is able to have entrepreneurial tendencies and hone their skills in meaningful ways. Matt Hansen's greatest strength is that he has a *diverse background of experiences* in the industry that gives him an understanding and ability to have discourse on most anything about the games development process. In a small team setting at Double Fine, Matt has an opportunity to take on new risks and challenges as an entrepreneur would but within the framework and security of working at an established company.

Although, the video game industry might be dominated largely by AAA-gaming with publishers such as Activision Blizzard, EA, and Ubisoft, there is a whole other level to gaming with independent game developers that makes them entrepreneurs. To quote Eric Koester:

> "My personal sense is that being an entrepreneur is very much a way of thinking and approach and is a way you live. It is this **insane curiosity**, *willingness to fail*, *willingness to try things*, and <u>basically never being satisfied with the status quo</u> – having this insatiable urge to understand."

Eric is saying is that being an entrepreneur comes largely down to how you view the world and your approach to the challenges that you face. Eric firmly believes that having curiosity, a willingness to try things and fail, and not settling for the status quo are integral to the entrepreneurial mindset and what it means to be an entrepreneur. When talking about an "insatiable urge to understand," Eric believes that someone who is entrepreneurial or an entrepreneur does not quite see the world the way everyone else does, and will always be asking "why."

The entrepreneur is someone who is always being called *crazy* by their friends because they are challenging the status quo by always doing something, creating, and sharing it with other people. Someone who acts like an entrepreneur is someone who will always want to know more and understand new ideas, because they always want to solve problems.

Gary Vaynerchuk, serial entrepreneur, CEO, author, public speaker, and Internet personality maintains:

> "I love the climb. I truly believe the definition of an entrepreneur is loving the process more than the things you get out of it."

In conjunction with Eric's thought on the entrepreneurial mindset and what it means to be an entrepreneur, it becomes very clear that being an entrepreneur means having an unquenchable desire to grow and challenge oneself. This is why Sean Vanaman left Telltale Games to co-found Campo Santo. In describing why he left Telltale to co-found Campo Santo, Sean wrote in one of Campo Santo's first blog posts that being able to pursue that process of creating something and challenge the status quo was like "winning the lottery."

In the case of Sean, leaving Telltale and being one of the creators of a new video game studio meant that he was able to pursue his passion of creating and telling stories. Within that is an authentic entrepreneur story. Sean as an entrepreneurial person honed his skills and talents at Telltale Games working on Telltale's The Walking Dead, all the while he had this desire to want to go out on his own and do something. Sean as an entrepreneur not only was one of the people who created an independent games studio (Campo Santo), he acted on his desire. If Sean had instead stayed at Telltale Games, Sean's story would be very different, but because he took action instead of standing on the sidelines, Sean, like other independent game developers, is an entrepreneur.

Gary Vaynerchuk, an immigrant from what is now Belarus, who is now a proud New Yorker, explained his perspective on his motivations as an entrepreneur, he said:

> "I don't like the stuff. I don't want watches. Fuck watches. I don't need planes. I don't need dick. **I need the process.**"

If Gary Vaynerchuk's name were replaced with Jonathan Blow's name, his perspective on money and material goods would be exactly the same. Jonathan, who spent three years making Braid, which he released in 2008, does not have a single business-centric bone in his body. Jonathan views money with apathy at best and antipathy at worst. For him, money signifies a *high score* in his bank account, which he only values insofar as it allows him to pursue his craft. Interchange Jonathan's name again with Gary Vaynerchuk and his love of the climb and how the continual process more than the results is indistinguishable. For all intents and purposes, Jonathan is an entrepreneur. Jonathan loves the act of creating video games, so much so that when he was finished with development on Braid he was $40,000 in debt. He might **not** be a *business person*, but he *is* an entrepreneur.

Scott Belsky, co-founder of Behance, an online platform for creative people to showcase their portfolios, said, "It's not about ideas. It's about making ideas happen."

John Erskine, VP of Publishing at Cloud Imperium Games and co-founder of both Portalarium and Rhino Moon Captioning, believes:

> "It's a hit driven entertainment based business, the nature of the work is very cyclical. As an entrepreneur, it's magnified because oftentimes you're the one that is responsible for the decisions that lead to consequences, consequences that happen to other people."

For John Erskine, founding a video game company and a full-service closed captioning, subtitling, and transcription studio, creating an independent game studio is exactly like creating a traditional start-up.

Much like in other industries, the business of video games is always changing. John Erskine, on this idea added:

> "Game companies are like a **rollercoaster ride**: you are either growing or shrinking – you are almost never just staying the same."

The parallels in this statement between an independent game developer studio and a start-up are uncanny. In the early stages of creating a company, time is of the essence to get your idea off the ground and prove its legitimacy.

Venture capitalists, when they evaluate whether or not to invest in a start-up idea consider the "Three Ts": 1) The Team, 2) **The Tech**, and 3) *The Traction*.

In applying this idea to indie gaming, the questions become:

- Who are the developers working on your project (is it a solo-effort or a team-effort)?
- What is your game concept and idea (how is your idea different, what is its entertainment value)?
- What concept art or prototype do you have for the game and what is the measured/anticipated interest in it?

Those in the indie gaming space need to ask and know the answers to these fundamental questions.

Yogventures, a video game envisioned by the popular YouTube channel Yogcast, although it made over $560,000 on Kickstarter, was cancelled in 2014 because development for the game was more complicated than expected. In the particular case of *Yogventures* there were problems with both "The Team" and "The Tech," because the development studio for the game, Winterkewl Games LLC, was shut down because the project was too much for them to handle. Yogcast's Lewis Brindley wrote, "The project was proving too ambitious and difficult for them to complete with their six-man team."

The Ouya, a video game console that received $8,596,474 in crowdfunding on Kickstarter, was a project in 2012 that promised to bring mobile gaming to the television. The Ouya was considered the fifth-highest earning project in Kickstarter history at the time, so there was a genuine crowdfunding interest to see the project come to life. The Ouya, when it was released in 2013 however, failed as a product because the larger consumer interest lacked a desire to play mobile games on a TV – that is what console gaming is for. They had sadly overlooked the traction part of the equation.

There is something to independent developers recognizing that they are entrepreneurs though. Independent developers as entrepreneurs are not simply a game designer, a programmer, an animator, an audio engineer, or a writer. Independent developers as entrepreneurs are not simply artists perfecting their art form of choice (video games), or creating entertainment to be consumed. Independent developers are creators of meaningful and enriching experiences for others. Notably, independent developers are innovators and pioneers who by the very act of making video games that can be played by hundreds, if not thousands or millions, of people are fostering a sense of community.

Eric Koester, when speaking on entrepreneurship, said, "Communities are not just made up of people starting a company, but also the people around them." Independent developers, if they recognize that they are entrepreneurs, are given a new power and new responsibility. By taking ownership of video games development as an indie developer, like an entrepreneur, the opportunities become limitless and so do the challenges.

Kickstarter or Indiegogo, which both have histories where games have been crowd funded and succeeded as well as failed, are no longer platforms where an indie developer is reliant on them as just a means to get funding. Crowd funding platforms, which have proven to be incredibly fickle with video games, take on new meaning in that they allow a developer to do more than showcase their idea, get the project off the ground, make the game, and then repeat the process. In taking crowdfunding as an approach to make a game that will ultimately be the basis for making a full-fledged independent development studio, a developer has much more potential at their fingertips. In the case of using crowdfunding, as an example of an indie developer seeing themselves as an artist versus entrepreneurs, crowdfunding either allows the developer to make a singular game or allows them to make a career out of their passion. It would be a false dichotomy to say that an indie developer is either an artist or an entrepreneur. An indie developer can be, and often is, both, which does not dilute the value of either the *artistry* or the *entrepreneurship* of the developer. Indie developers are both an artist and an entrepreneur at the same time, and they are all the better for it. This idea elevates their status as an independent developer and better informs their opportunities for growth and success.

This distinction, an indie developer recognizing their entrepreneurial tendencies, does not mean that they will eventually become like "an evil corporation." Matt Hansen, who has spoken to a great number of students who want to one day enter the video game industry, observed that the video game industry is going through a "weird era" because students have a skewed perspective on how the industry works, especially on the difference between AAA games and indie development. Matt Hansen, through his own experiences, has found that students turn their nose up to AAA because that is the "evil part of the industry," and that they would rather adventure out and do indie projects either solo or with friends. But the problem for these students arises when it becomes apparent that they lack the experience to actually be successful independent developers, like Mark Cooke (CEO of Shiny Shoe), let alone at the level of Markus Persson (*Minecraft*).

The parallels between entrepreneurship and the video game industry become even clearer in light of Matt Hansen's observations. Eric Koester, in his lecture of "Living in the Era of Entrepreneurship," noted, more people are hungry for the "entrepreneurial life," and that a study has shown 70% of millennials want to be entrepreneurs. But, as Eric pointed out, "just 11% of all Americans work for themselves (and less than that for millennials)."

Even if one doubles the 11% to 22% that still suggests that most individuals are not working for themselves. As the Founder Fallacy goes, college dropouts are not starting most companies, and, in fact, the average founder age is 40. The average founder age in the video game industry may be lower, and getting lower with increased ease of access to technology but sequencing of experience, first established company then independent, this sequencing seems significant in the video game industry. Matt Hansen and John Erskine both echoed the notion by arguing that the most successful independent game developers are the ones who enter the indie gaming scene after getting some level of industry experience.

Mark Cooke exemplifies how industry experience made his endeavor to create Shiny Shoe a viable idea. Before founding

Shiny Shoe, he pursued a career path at Nihilistic Software. Upon being asked if he thought he was an entrepreneur, Mark responded:

> "I don't know. Yes, I do. Because I'm trying to get a business off the ground, and it's independent, I guess so. It's not just something I think about."

That is why an independent developer must see himself or herself as an entrepreneur. By recognizing oneself as an entrepreneur, it elevates their identity, their playing field and gives them a framework for how to view the world.

Eric Koester has described the Entrepreneur's Journey as such:

> Inspiration Learning Tribe Intra-(preneurship) Entre-(preneurship)

But the problem is, when an independent developer does not necessarily view themselves as an entrepreneur, or when a student wants to be an indie developer but lacks the experience, they fall into the path of a **wantrapeneur**. That is the term that Eric uses to describe the 70% of millennials who want to be entrepreneurs but don't know how to be. But the reason someone is a *wantrapreneur* and pursues the path of entrepreneurship, is they have a dream of some kind.

The first step of the Entrepreneur's Journey is to have an inspiration of some kind that engages and sparks curiosity. Assuming the curiosity is strong enough, that person will want to pursue that passion, to learn more and dialogue with the inspiration however they can (e.g., read books and articles, go to school, speak to experts and potential customers, etc.). From there, a successful entrepreneur on their journey must surround themselves with like-minded people, who also want to be entrepreneurs one day, or will help and support you in some way (e.g., allies, drinking buddies, partners in crime, etc.). These connections are the one that will help to sustain the passion. The most important stage before someone completes the Entrepreneur's Journey and becomes a true entrepreneur is to be intrapreneurial. Once you have an understanding of intrapreneurship (entrepreneurial activities in the context of a larger organization), through innovation training of some sort, you can begin working on projects that hone and polish your skills. There is no substitute for doing.

Efficiency projects, cost cutting projects, and revenue optimizing projects, which you might consider consulting projects are all internal innovation projects. As a successful intrapreneur, you must have the expertise to explore, optimize, and scale, and thereby start a new business system or product. In effect, you can start a business and more likely to be successful because you have skills and expertise. You have a toolbox filled with some tools to pull out and use. This is because the person who wants to be an independent developer, a *wantrapreneur*, will have developed a pathway to be an entrepreneur.

The Entrepreneur's journey explains the potential that exists for an independent developer when they recognize that they are entrepreneur. According to Marc Merrill (Co-Founder of Riot Games), valuing developers, in this case independent developers, is the key to unlocking the next level of the video game industry. This idea comes back to the fact that if indie developers are seen as more than artists, as both artists and entrepreneurs, the world becomes their oyster. This recognition unlocks a potential to understand and better appreciate the lessons and values of working in the video game industry in a way that has not been done.

KEY INSIGHTS AND TAKEAWAY LESSONS

- People think that all indie developers can make it big if they act like Markus "Notch" Persson, but the truth is he is the Mark Zuckerberg of gaming (i.e. a Unicorn)
- Indie developers (video game entrepreneurs) are pursuing their path for the same reasons as any entrepreneur does, which means that if they started acting like the entrepreneurs that they are and not just game developers, they could gain a competitive edge.
- Indie developers who live and breathe the Entrepreneur's Journey are more likely to succeed where others have failed.

- The Entrepreneurs Journey: "Inspiration Learning Tribe Intra Entre"

ADDITIONAL INDUSTRY VETERAN PERSPECTIVE:

"Indie developers are following a passion for a game or a genre and want to work on that game with more freedom then they would be allowed in a larger enterprise. Many of the Indie game studios don't remain indie forever and they eventually grow into a larger company with all of the benefits. Then the cycle starts again!"

— BLAKE EDWARDS (PLAYER RELATIONS

SPECIALIST, RIOT GAMES)

"It's about the iterative process and it's incredibly healthy. And then you go through polish time when you polish that feature, you refine that feature and make it sing. The trouble comes when you reach a point that when you realize no matter what polish you put in, it's going to be wrong."

— PETER MOLYNEUX (FOUNDER, LIONHEAD

STUDIOS AND 22CANS)

PART 3

TAKING
ACTION

CHAPTER 6

FINDING YOUR TRIBE: WHY NETWORKING AND MENTORSHIP MAKES ALL THE DIFFERENCE

"An enduring problem with any business of finding great people. You can have the most genius idea in the world but if you don't have a team to execute that idea it isn't worth anything."

— PETER MOLYNEUX (CREATOR OF FABLE, FOUNDER

OF LIONHEAD STUDIOS AND 22CANS)

CHAPTER FOCUS:

- Examination on the Video Game Industry Culture as it relates to Networking and Community
- Highlighting How everyone in the Video Game Industry knows each other and Why that Matters
- Conversation on the many ways people in the Industry want to help and empower each other through Community
- How Mentorship is effective for Personal and Professional Development

"It all comes down to the most difficult part — getting to know the right people and that comes from talking and communicating." With humble beginnings, having attended GDC in March 2010, David Voyles saw that through networking and finding people with common interests and passions, he was able to create not just a name for himself, but also a community that he could rely on no matter the circumstances.

David Voyles is not a traditional software engineer, game designer, or indie game developer – he has a background in Communications from State University of New York College at Oneonta, and is a self-proclaimed "construction worker and self-taught software engineer." One might think that such an unorthodox background might make difficult for David to thrive in the video game industry. What allowed David to thrive is that he cares about people, and in the grand scheme of things, that is a defining feature of what has made David so successful in the indie games space.

David found that in prioritizing the development of honest, authentic relationships and having that sense of community, he was able to surround himself with people who could help him grow professionally in terms of constructive criticism, ideation, and networking. David channeled his energies here because he knew that in having a genuine interest in other people and what they were passionate about, which coincidentally lined up with a passion of his (**spoiler**: the answer is video games), it would be a good idea all the way around.

David through his experiences came up with the idea to create Armless Octopus, a podcast that highlights indie developers. Along with a couple of friends, a merry band of misfits, David set himself on a journey to cover video game industry news in a new light. Armless Octopus' goal was to showcase the video game industry in a way that not many people had been doing at the time, because it would give a voice to indie developers and their craft. Nowadays, video game media and journalism is starting to cover indie titles and developers left and right.

But David Voyles was one of the few people who led the charge on this effort before it was *cool*.

Yet how did he manage it? It all goes back to the fact that David Voyles surrounded himself with people who he could engage with and be empowered by as he did the same for them, and a sense of community followed from there. In turn, when all was said and done, David reflected on his experiences and discerned what it all meant for him, and thus he was able to find his voice.

Community is the most defining aspect of the video game industry, especially in the indie gaming community. David Voyles is but one of the many people who have found how influential community is as it relates to working in the video game industry. Community is invaluable in the video game industry as a whole, but it takes on a whole new meaning in the indie gaming space. This is essential to understand because in the video game industry, everyone knows each other. Moreover, everyone in the video game industry wants to develop meaningful relationships with one another, as well as create new and different types of communities. This is true for whomever you talk to, practically anybody in the video game industry. This notion especially holds true for the most innovative, creative, and dynamic figures in the industry because for them it is about passing on their knowledge to the future generations of game developers by paying it forward. Since community is important as it is in the video game industry, *tribe building* is both a necessity and an asset if it is done right.

Everyone has a passion for what they are doing and they

want to support others as they pursue their craft. In a lot of ways, indie gaming is like the music scene in that everyone is collaborating with and rivaling against one another in a Battle of the Bands competition to create the next breakout indie game. The musicians (indie developers) are creating their own music (indie games) either in bands (small teams) or as a solo artist (individual developer) and they all want to live a life where they are living out a culture of creativity and innovation. But the way that they are able to accomplish this is through perfecting their art form by making fun and exciting new games.

These indie developers might not have the budgets of their AAA-counterparts, but they have an internal motivation to pursue their craft in any way that they know how, and one of the ways that they are able to accomplish this is through fostering a sense of community.

In the video game industry, almost everyone knows each other in some way or another. Almost every social and professional network in the industry is interconnected in some way. Mark Cooke, Founder and CEO of Shiny Shoe, is great friends with Matt Hansen, the COO at Double Fine Productions. Their friendship goes quite a way back, and relationships like theirs are what make the video game industry inviting to other people. Mark and Matt have worked together in the video game industry because Double Fine Productions has hired

Shiny Shoe on a number of occasions to work on different projects. As a result of these professional and personal relationships, it becomes commonplace for bonds to form that result in creating multi-layered communities.

Matt Hansen, before he worked at Double Fine Productions, the acclaimed video game developer, known for *Psychonauts* (2005), which received a BAFTA video game Best Screen Play Award, founded by Tim Schafer in 2000, worked at Telltale Games. In taking a step back, Double Fine and Telltale are both spin-offs of LucasArts, the video game subsidiary of LucasFilm. What's more, Matt Hansen, before he joined the team at Double Fine knew several people at Double Fine who he talked to when he considered making the switch between companies. The reason that switch was made possible and a feasible transition is because Matt had already personally known people at Double Fine. This might seem surprising, but this is far from the exception in the video game industry culture, it is the rule. Even if someone does not know someone else personally, they have likely at least heard of the person's name and some of their work, and, more likely, know someone who knows them. Crossover in the video game industry like Matt Hansen and Mark Cooke, as well as Double Fine Productions and Telltale Games is what differentiates the video game industry from most other industries.

When talking about why he wanted to leave Telltale for Double

Fine, Matt explained that he was drawn in by the personality of Tim Schafer and his creative vision for the company. Matt explained that he enjoyed working on Adventure Games at Telltale, but he was excited that after *Brütal Legend* (2009), a AAA game made by the privately-owned company, Double Fine would be making a shift towards smaller ideas and projects. The reason this excited Matt is that to him smaller projects translated to more creativity and dynamism because working on smaller teams meant a greater individual impact on the part of each individual team member. For Matt, in moving to Double Fine he found exactly what he wanted: an opportunity to take his broad understanding as a producer in games development and be challenged in new ways while getting to know the people on his team in a deeper, more meaningful way.

At the AAA-level, developers will know the people on their team, but will probably not know that many people beyond that, because video games development is siloed, especially when the larger team as a whole is 200+ employees strong. At Double Fine, however, there are only 65 employees at the company, so the culture is vastly different than working at a traditional company such as EA or Ubisoft.

In considering the larger video game industry, there is a greater sense of community that exists. Rich Vogel and Gordon Walton, two video game industry veterans, with close to sixty years of experience between them both, their friendship illustrates how strong the bonds the video game industry can get:

- Rich Vogel and Gordon Walton both worked at Origin Systems, founded by Richard Garriott, from 1997 to 2000 as a Senior Producer and 1999 to 2001 VP Online and Executive Producer respectively.
- Rich Vogel worked at Sony Online Entertainment as the studio General Manager and Executive Producer of *Star Wars Galaxies* (a Star Wars MMORPG) from 2000 to 2005
- Gordon Walton was an Executive Producer and Studio Manager from 2003 to 2005
- From there, both Rich Vogel and Gordon Walton left Sony Online Entertainment to found and Co-Studio Direct and Manage the BioWare Austin Studio to develop *Star Wars: The Old Republic*, the newest Star Wars MMORPG.
- Rich Vogel's tenure there lasted from 2005 to 2012, first as Co-Studio Director and then Executive Producer, and Gordon Walton worked at BioWare Austin from 2005 to 2011.

Rich Vogel and Gordon Walton's friendship was more than just a working dynamic. They were, as Gordon put it, "partners." In talking about why they both started the BioWare Austin Studio and worked on Star Wars: The Old Republic, Gordon said:

"After leaving them (Sony Online Entertainment) I started

looking for my next opportunity. My partner Rich Vogel left about two months after I did so we started looking for where we thought there was maybe one last big MMO that could be done before the free to play thing took over. That was kind of our premise is that there might be room for one bigger MMO."

Rich Vogel and Gordon Walton were not just partners who worked on the same projects throughout their career: they were on the same team. This mentality in particular is what many video game developers feel towards their colleagues. Developers might only work together for a couple of months or a year or two together, in the case of Rich and Gordon it was over many years and on many different projects.

In the process of working closely together, over long work weeks and for such prolonged periods of time, developers start to feel as though they are more than friends: they are *foxhole buddies*. Any video game is a gargantuan undertaking to accomplish, and it requires a great deal of effort, time, and resources in order to make for a great game. The game, when it is completed, it quite literally is a war that has been won on the side of the developers. Thus, when developers talk about their relationships with one another, they are illuminating the authenticity of the bonds and community that they have formed.

When talking further about Rich, Gordon said:

> "Oh, we're like an old married couple. We have worked together, off and on for ten years. So, we know each other well. We know each other's strengths and weaknesses. We argue and bitch at each other all the time but we get stuff done. That would be the way I would describe us. I just saw him at lunch yesterday. … Rich is a very creative, very smart guy, so he's got a lot of talent, a lot of raw talent and a lot of smarts…"

At the time, Gordon said that (2013), he and Rich were at very different places. Based out of Austin, Texas, they were always a stone's throw away. Gordon had left Playdom, a now defunct studio that had been bought by Disney Interactive (the games subsidiary of Disney), to found ArtCraft Entertainment, Inc., a video game start-up, interested in pushing the boundaries of online gaming. Rich Vogel, on the other hand, had become President of Battlecry Studios, a studio under Bethesda Softworks. Although their paths have separated since 2011, their bond represents the overall sense of community and investment people in the video game industry have towards each other.

In addition to everyone knowing each other, people in the video game industry want to help and empower others in meaningful ways. In the case of Matt Hansen, he is a strong proponent of Double Fine's approach to empowering others as a means to develop community, especially independent game developers. In a portion of Double Fine Production's office spaces, Double Fine rents out the space to indie developers, specifically award winning teams who make award-winning games. Double Fine believes in this because they want to act as an incubator, a safe space of sorts, to allow these small indie developer teams, typically 1-2 people in size, to do what they do best. The reason for this is although these indie developers are award winning and their game(s) reflect their talent, the success that these games achieved is not always sufficient to allow the developers to sustain themselves.

In the video game industry, most especially at the indie-level, making a critically acclaimed game might not result in a breakout hit with millions of dollars worth of sales; Braid and Minecraft are but two of the handful of exceptions to this rule. Therefore, it becomes all the more important for indie developers to cut costs wherever they can, and workspace is one such example. Double Fine Productions offers this space to alleviate this particular pressure point that indie developers feel and are able to grant a reprieve to a lucky few, and that makes all the difference for those developers.

But empowerment in the video game industry goes beyond companies such as Double Fine creating an incubator-space for indie developers. Sonja Ängeslevä, Product Director at Unity

Technologies, who is based out of Helsinki, Finland, has found her work as a mentor for GameFounders quite meaningful. GameFounders, a global game studio incubator, was founded for the purpose of connecting independent game developers with interested mentors in the video game industry from around the world. The goal of a GameFounder mentor is to provide their mentees with mentorship and help them wade through their endeavors to be successful independent game developers. Game studios that are selected by GameFounders not only receive expert mentorship, they also receive funding and other support to drive growth. In reflecting on one of her experiences as a mentor for GameFounders, for which she is still a part of, Sonja, wrote:

> "I am specialized in community activations and user gener-
> ated content but the OneEyeAnt guys were brilliant. They
> had original approaches to user acquisition. After our
> session, I felt that they got something out of the session,
> but so did I. That was a very inspiring moment to me."

Much like mentorship in any context, GameFounders allows mentors and mentees to learn from one another and develop friendships that create larger communities. GameFounders allows indie developers from around the world to interact with mentors from across the world, which in turn creates a worldwide gaming community that has far reaching implications. There are merits to Double Fine's approach as well as at

GameFounders, but what both accomplish is a greater sense of togetherness and camaraderie between indie developers.

There is also a push in the video game industry on the part of industry veterans who want to create new kinds of video game industry communities. Guha Bala and Karthik Bala are brothers who founded Vicarious Visions, a New York based video game development studio, in 1990 while they were still in high school. Vicarious Visions is a development studio that is most notable for their work on handheld games. Vicarious Visions became known as the leading developer of handheld games through their work on:

- *Tony Hawk's Pro Skater Series*, which they developed for every Gameboy Advance and Nintendo DS title version
- Several *Spider-Man* games
- The first three *Crash Bandicoot* Gameboy Advance games
- *Guitar Hero* on the Nintendo DS and the Wii
- *Skylanders*.

Vicarious Visions has received a litany of awards from media outlets for their work (2000-2010). Most of all, Vicarious Visions was bought by Activision in January 2005.

More recently, in April 2016, Guha and Karthik announced that they were leaving Vicarious Visions to go find a new studio. When Guha and Karthik left Vicarious Visions, they created Velan Studios (Troy, New York). Velan Studios, according to the Bala Brothers:

> "Is an independent video game developer focused on developing innovative, experimental games using new technology such as virtual reality, sensor technology, new platforms and more."

The main purpose of creating their studio in New York is they want to hire industry veterans and bring them into the New York region and then pair them up with new talent from such as Rensselaer Polytechnic Institute, Rochester, and NYU. The Bala Brothers recognized that the video game industry is largely based out of Los Angeles and San Francisco, California and Austin, Texas. The Bala Brothers believe that in pursuing this venture to the fullest extent, they might be able to make upstate New York a new video game industry heartland. Like many indie developers who have left the AAA-space, they created their studio because they have a desire to go back to their small team roots and in the process, work on new and innovative technologies. Velan Studios operates under Velan Ventures, a venture investment firm focused on gaming and digital entertainment companies, which, much like their effort to bring in industry veterans and empower recent college grads, is based in the spirit of fostering a culture of games development.

Community, regardless of what form it takes, matters in the video game industry. People know each other and they place a great deal of emphasis and value on developing not only great games but also life-long friendships and networks. This mindset is one of the most defining aspects of the video game industry, and in the indie gaming scene it is all the more present and valuable.

Networking and community is how indie developers go from: working on a solo project to working on a team, getting constructive feedback to receiving insights that revolutionize a game concept, and having colleagues to having allies and confidants. The video game industry revels in community in every facet of its culture, and gaming culture mirrors this. Without community, independent game developers would not be the innovators that they are.

Community and networking are the two biggest *assets* for an independent developer. In order to survive, let alone thrive, it is a necessity for an independent developer to reach out and get to know others, to cultivate positive working relationships. Gordon Walton and Rich Vogel are a great example of this, because not only have they been great work colleagues, they are even better friends. It would be transactional to say that it kills two birds with one stone to know people that are both friends and network opportunities to promote a game. But that is not what good network and community is all about, if the sentiments of David Voyles, the Bala Brothers, and Sonja Ängeslevä are to be believed. Surrounding oneself around people with the same interests and desires to grow and succeed, to find a tribe, is of the upmost importance for the budding indie entrepreneur. On the Entrepreneur's Journey, as an independent game developer, it is not enough to have the inspiration to be entrepreneur and always be learning new things. It does not matter the size, shape, or form the tribe takes on: what matters is that a tribe exists and that it is blossoming into a wonderful community and network of friends, drinking buddies, and allies who will support each other throughout their respective journeys – these are a handful of ways that they can form in the video game industry.

KEY INSIGHTS AND TAKEAWAY LESSONS

- Community is everything in the video game industry. Everyone knows each other, and people want to help others succeed and accomplish great things – so reach out and build your network.
    - If you don't know where to start, talk about the one thing you know for certain they would be open to talking about (video games)
    - Build connections for life, not just for the moment.
- Indie developers (video game entrepreneurs) should actively pursue in the act of "Tribe Building", i.e. authentic relationships.
    - Whether they be work colleagues, friends, family, mentors, drinking buddies, etc. they are a necessary ally to help you

on your journey as an entrepreneur in the video game industry

- Seek out a mentor
- Mentor others as well

ADDITIONAL INDUSTRY VETERAN PERSPECTIVE:

"Once you are in, attitude and relationships are everything. Don't think anything or anyone is beneath you, because over time you'll move around and other people do too, so personal references will be critical to your advancement."

— JOHN ERSKINE (VP OF PUBLISHING, CLOUD IMPERIUM GAMES)

"The best team is a mix of people who have no experience whatsoever. So when setbacks first happen they just think that this is the way it works. Mixed with people with a high degree of experience to help guide them. So pulling a team together and getting them to accept that failure of things."

— PETER MOLYNEUX (FOUNDER, LIONHEAD STUDIOS AND 22CANS)

CHAPTER 7

LESSONS FROM VIDEO GAME ENTREPRENEURS

"Look at the situation as it currently exists. I never allow, "it would be nice", "we could have, should have". I always look at what it is right now."

— JENNIFER BULLARD (DIRECTOR OF PROGRAM
MANAGEMENT, QUERIUM CORPORATION)

CHAPTER FOCUS:

- The Challenges of creating a start-up in the Video Game Industry

- Applying the skills of Entrepreneurship when making an Indie Game and creating a sustainable business model
- Exploration of what it means to Learn from failure in the Video Game Industry
- Why iteration and time management are an Indie Developer's Best Friends
- Taking what you have learned as a "wantrapreneur" and becoming a full-fledged entrepreneur

"'Let's just stop talking for a second and appreciate the fact that we're doing this.' We're really doing it. Every once in a while we have that moment. It's easy to keep your head down and just go 20 hours a day [appreciating it]." Paul Trowe, CEO of Replay Games Inc., spoke about his philosophy on games development in an interview with Digital Trends (2013). Paul developed this philosophy on game design when he was on a walk with a colleague, and it has informed his appreciation for what he is able to do as someone in the video game industry ever since.

When Paul and his colleague were taking a break one day from a conference that they were at, they came across a garden, and his friend told him that he wanted to stop there for a moment. The garden, filled with a variety of flowers that made for a vibrant yet relaxing stop, was where he had his first encounter with this philosophy.

In the video game industry, moments such as these are learning opportunities. Every success and failure is predicated upon those moments where invaluable lessons are experienced and codified. Therefore, it is not enough to accept the fact that independent game developers are entrepreneurs and that they are exceptionally well positioned to redefine the video game industry. Because independent game developers are entrepreneurs, the principles of entrepreneurship and their associated lessons are applicable to almost every facet of an indie developer's life. This chapter is a compilation of a number of thoughts that video game developers, both AAA and Indie, have for the would-be entrepreneur who wants to enter the video game industry as an indie developer:

- Time management
- Compensation
- The value of teaching others
- Having clear audience vision
- Central role of risk taking.

Time management can make or break if a video game launches on time and as a finished project. It is a two-fold issue in that it is both important to make sure time is managed such that developers do not fall behind on deadlines, which result in project delays, and that both timelines, cost and quality are maximized. More and more in the video game industry, video games are not launching as complete games. Brian Crecente, an executive editor at Polygon, an American video game website owned by Vox Media, wrote:

> "Today's cutting edge of game consoles brought with them living worlds, new ways to interact with entertainment and experiences that weave seamlessly with vast social networks. They also created a new norm: Selling not a finished game, but the promise of one."

Brian Crecente wrote that article in November 2014, and his words still ring true today: video games are not being sold at launch as company leadership promise at the start. *Assassin's Creed Unity*, a game that was also released in 2014, is a game that gamers will often point to, to highlight this idea. When *Assassin's Creed Unity*, which was a game developed by Ubisoft Montreal as the lead studio on the project and published by Ubisoft, was released, the game was unplayable. From graphics glitches to gameplay mechanics not working, *Assassin's Creed Unity* highlighted how modern games companies were struggling to match quality given the time that they would have developers spend on making games.

This is not surprising to anyone in the video game industry or to someone who understands the work culture in the industry. In the video game industry, there is something known as *crunch time*. Certain games companies more so than others, but prevalent nonetheless across the video game industry, relied on overtime as a means to make up for failing to meet milestones or grapple with an increasingly complicated work flow. Crunch time, though is more than *overtime*, it is overtime on steroids because teams end up doing this for prolonged periods of time, on the order of several months, especially towards the end of a project timeline. Some systematic changes have been made, especially at the larger, publicly traded companies such as EA, but it is still an issue that raises the important issue of how to manage a project.

Although independent game developers are not working on this scale, if they make use of various marketing tools that be (news outlets, crowdfunding, social media), they are forced in some way or another to release a project by a certain time and date. Delays are permissible, which are common especially in the AAA, but when it comes from an unproven developer or a studio with a mixed history in making great games it can spell doom for the game. An example where a delay was much needed was with *The Witcher 3: The Wild Hunt*, which won Game of the Year and Best RPG at many awards shows and by many critics, but this is not always the case.

Therefore, it is important to keep in mind the value in setting goals that take into account potential challenges or roadblocks that would delay the project in some way.

Jennifer Bullard, Director of Program Management at Querium

Corporation and a Women in Power Finalist in the Austin Business Journal, when talking about project management said, "It's human nature to overlook the things you don't want to do." In Jennifer's experience, this is one key way in which project timelines can be skewed or idealistic as opposed to realistic in terms of practicality.

Reflecting on this further, Jennifer told a story about how she had a conversation with a colleague about a feature they wanted to introduce. Her immediate reaction was to ask them how long they thought it would take, and they replied that it would take, "2 weeks to implement the idea."

Jennifer, a savvy video game developer, quickly discerned that it was important to, "understand when someone is being overly optimistic." She had her colleague go back and specifically name every single step and thing that would need to be done to implement their idea and how long it would take for them to do each thing. The colleague did the math and realized that, "instead of taking 2 weeks, it would take 9 months."

The gut check this employee had was far off the mark. Jennifer was able to hone her scheduling methods through her experiences and the experiences of her mentors, which is why she believes it is important to share her knowledge with others.

Mark Cooke of Shiny Shoe, when talking about how he goes

about project management and scheduling ideas, he does a very similar process, but because he has a great deal of experience in the industry, he does not need to manually write everything down in an excel spreadsheet; his experience allows him to more quickly do the math in his head. The bottom line though, no matter how you go about scheduling out a project, it is important to have a schedule and to consider in as holistic a way as possible the implications of every decision and what it would have on the overall timeline. And then add contingency on top of those calculations. More often than not a feature will need to be added or some other kind of modification that will require reworking entire large portions of the product.

Another key thing to keep top of mind is how the project you are working on is being funded. As an entrepreneur, an independent developer needs to consider if they are self-funding, crowdfunding, signing a publishing deal, or working with a venture capitalist to cover development costs. Most of the time in the video game industry, independent developers either self-fund a game or go the route of crowdfunding.

The reason against a publishing deal is publishers often in a written contract create restrictions of some kind on the independent developer that either strip the developer of their rights to the IP or force the game to go in a different, undesired direction. It also creates handcuffs of sort in dealing with issues and opportunities as they arise while developing the project.

In the case of venture capital, independent developers do not see venture capitalists as a traditional form of funding, especially when compared to crowdfunding platforms like Kickstarter and Indiegogo. Due to the fact that indie developers are entrepreneurs, venture capital can and should become a more viable pathway to create a business around the game, especially when considering the fact that venture capitalists and angel investors have the business experience that can help get the business (independent development studio) surrounding the game off the ground as a full-fledged company. Complications can arise, just as with a publishing deal, but that comes down to looking at the fine print of the contract and knowing what is getting agreed to between both parties.

In the video game industry AAA-space, compensation, depending on the company might be a certainty or it might not be. Demetrius Comes, a former Executive Director of Engineering at WB Games – Turbine, reflected on his time as Vice President of Technology at Cheyenne Mountain Entertainment (CME), the company behind the *Stargate Worlds* MMO, a game that has never been released. *Stargate Worlds* was never released because CME experienced financial troubles, in the way of compensation, which forced layoffs. In commenting on this happening, which was roughly in 2008-2009, Demetrius said:

"We were supposed to get paid two weeks later, but the paychecks didn't show, and were three days late. Then roughly from August until late October paychecks were there, they were just offset by a week. So rather than getting paid when we were supposed to, we got paid the following Friday. Basically, everyone was running a week behind payroll wise. After the initial shock of that, by the second week of September, things started getting back to normal."

In November, however, paychecks stopped completely, and people started leaving the company because although they wanted to see the game through to the end, family came first. Demetrius said:

> "*Everybody believed*: If we just got it out the door we'd be successful."

Although the belief was there, it never came to fruition and CME was forced to close its doors and layoff its employees. Indie developers might not be working on a comparable scale to a AAA-company, but Demetrius' story nevertheless highlights the importance of valuing money as both a means to fund the game as well as compensation for one's own personal life as well as those on the team. It might be possible for some developers to rely on living in their parents' house, or finding a comparable way to cut costs, save money, and be able to survive, but strategies such as those are not a guarantee nor are they usually a long-term strategy. Therefore, in order to be a successful indie developer, it is important to think like an entrepreneur would when it comes to funding and paying for one's own expenses, whether it be having food on the table or taking care of one's family.

As an *entrepreneur*, it is important for an indie developer to teach others as well as be taught by others. Whether it is direct mentorship or creating a "How-To Guide", teaching as a means to grow and be a successful entrepreneur is key. David Voyles, a former Senior Software Engineer at Comcast, now a Senior Technical Evangelist, has a philosophy when it came to doing something: you might not know everything so asked for help if needed, and create systems that allow those that come after you to learn as well. When David was at Comcast, he was the sole developer on the Xfinity app for the Xbox One. A major task, especially considering it could potentially be used by millions of users, David realized early on:

> "I knew a lot of this work, that I could pick things up quickly, then it wasn't so bad. As long as you are honest with people, I'm in over my head, and then it's not so bad because you know you can go ask for help if you needed it."

David, like many in the video game industry believe that asking for help and getting mentorship or guidance in some way is a net benefit because in the long run it will allow you to develop skills and talents that will enable you to better succeed in the future. When David left Comcast, his replacement picked up exactly where he left off, and he was able to for two reasons:

- When David's replacement first started, David returned the following week to teach the new programmer what he had done
- David had taken a copious amount of notes and in effect had created a "How-To Guide" for his replacement to follow to the letter.

The purpose of both of those efforts on the part of David was to allow his replacement to understand where David ran into troubles as well as have a set of basic tips and tricks to help make people's jobs easier in the future.

Jennifer Bullard, when talking about the importance of teaching others said:

> "I focused on helping people that are disadvantaged with whatever information or knowledge that I have. Whether it was disadvantaged children that don't have access to college educated adults. I have also done some coaching and mentoring for those coming into the industry, to encourage women and minorities to enter because diversity definitely helps projects. The best video games are

when the team has been culturally diverse. A large part of it was just passing along my good fortune."

In a nutshell, this is why mentorship and guidance matters as both an indie developer and an entrepreneur. If not for this type of leadership, Jennifer might never have been set on the path that she was to be recognized as a Woman in Power Finalist in the Austin Business Journal, which is but one of her many major accomplishments. Because the video game industry is community-centric, teaching others is also a way to develop relationships that will empower an indie developer by creating allies and supporters who will be able to help later on in the future.

As an *entrepreneur*, having a clear vision for what you are creating, for who and why are crucial to know - both upfront and throughout the process. Peter Molyneux said:

"The biggest lesson: You have to think about your audience, who's going to play the game, who you want to play the game. Make sure you remind yourself of that as you go through development."

Peter Molyneux, the famed developer behind *Fable*, a cultural icon developed at Lionhead Studios, which was shut down in April 2016, and Founder and Creative Director of 22Cans (an indie studio in the UK). It is one thing to take on a complicated feature for a game if it is clear that gamers will make use of it, but it is another to stay true to the audiences wants and needs for a game and following that through to fruition.

Risk taking is a critical concept to understand as well – both one's tolerance for risk and potential that risk taking unlocks. When talking about how he learned about risk, Peter spoke about how since he has "flopped" between both AAA gaming and indie gaming throughout his career he developed awareness.

In speaking about why he left Microsoft to found 22Cans, Peter talked about his fascination with both the high score one could achieve with regard to one's bank account as well as risk. Peter explained that risk and creative license were defining factors for him, above money:

> "In the corporate world, that is what I missed the most, this sense of risk. The sense of taking a risk and jumping blindly into the black void and just hoping there is something down there below. That sense of risk, of pushing yourself, of pushing your team which may in a corporate sense seem almost insane. It's certainly not viable in business terms as a great catalyst for creativity and for making things that simply would never have existed if they had come from a corporate world."

Peter, as both an innovator and entrepreneur, admitted, as many other developers do, that risk is a clear distinction between the corporate world and indie gaming. Peter did not dismiss the corporate world though; he merely enjoyed the game that is entrepreneurship too much. Ironically, Peter, in his early days as a developer, created a game called The Entrepreneur (a business simulation game). The game did not fair very well in the market, and he often jokes (firmly believes) that of the two copies he sold, one of them was likely to his mother. Regardless of failure, Peter understood that he enjoyed the sense of risk and the ownership that came from taking on that degree of responsibility. Therefore, as an *entrepreneur* in the indie game understanding one's own aversion or proclivity towards risk is tantamount when it comes to succeeding. At the same time, Peter, although he had *failed*, kept making video games and stayed on his path – he would not let his dream of being a video game developer die.

With risk comes the potential for failure, as Peter said:

> "It sounds like a terrible thing because it sounds like failure but you have to accept that failure is a crucial part of the creative process. Without accepting failure, embracing failure and always hoping for failure, you are always going to struggle with creating something innovative."

Failure however does not have to necessary be a problem, it

can be a tool that is used to spur on newer ideas or success later on because as a developer you know where the mistakes can happen and can prevent them from happing again. In speaking on failure, Peter also said:

> "The best team includes a mix of people who have no experience whatsoever. So when setbacks first happen they just think that this is the way it works. Then mix in people with a high degree of experience to help guide them. So, pulling a team together and getting them to accept that failure of things."

To Peter, failure is **not** a *bad thing*: in fact it is the exact opposite. The learning curve brought on by failure when encountered by a team allows the team to grow and be more dynamic. The diversity and experience of a team is paramount to success, and in a start-up environment such as indie gaming, a team can make or break the quality of the end results. This was a large part of the reasoning that Peter had when he originally founded Lionhead Studios and then more recently with 22Cans. When you bring a diverse group of people together, who want to pursue great ideas and innovation, all in the desire to take on risk, you have the potential to see a lot of great things happen.

That is not to say making games in any capacity, by way of AAA or indie is easy. Feargus Urquhart, Founder and CEO of Obsidian Entertainment echoed this by saying:

> "Making games is probably one of the hardest things to do because every time you're making a new game, it has to look better, play better, and function better. We were all making Xbox 360 games for something like ten years and it didn't really change but somehow everybody was still expecting every game to be better."

Feargus' words speak to why it is salient to understand lessons of entrepreneurship before taking on responsibility as an entrepreneur in indie gaming. This is why, Feargus also noted, not taking responsibility and having others lead the way might not necessary a bad thing, "The biggest thing about being a dependent is that there are times that you have to be on the hamster wheel."

Being on the hamster wheel, according to Feargus is a double-edged sword, in that on the one hand it means your work is never finished, but on the other it means that you do not have much responsibility beyond doing your work to the best of your ability. If someone else fails and the project gets delayed, as the developer on the hamster wheel, especially in a corporate setting, it is not directly your fault. However, as an entrepreneur in indie gaming, a project delay falls on you either as an extra cost of time or financial risk associated with the project.

According to John Erskine, VP of Publishing at Clouding Imperium Games:

> "Game companies are like a roller-coaster ride, you are either growing or shrinking, you are almost never just staying the same."

As an entrepreneur in indie gaming, this statement rings true especially so. The risk one takes on as an entrepreneur, let alone in a dynamic and ever changing industry like the video game industry, forces the issue of risk even more.

These lessons of entrepreneurship from industry veterans and independent developers showcase how entrepreneurship is inextricably linked to indie gaming in a variety of different ways. Eric Koester, Founder & Chief Instigator at Kingmaker Labs, conveys this best when talking about the differences between an *entrepreneur* and a *wantrapreneur*. In listening to industry veterans and pioneers in the video game industry, entrepreneurs in indie gaming will be all the less likely to fall into the trap of being a "wantrapreneur." The end goal of an independent developer is to pursue their craft and make enjoyable games. In placing value in these lessons of entrepreneurs, independent developers are all the more well positioned to succeed and take over the video game industry and bring about the domination of indie gaming.

KEY INSIGHTS AND TAKEAWAY LESSONS

- Video game entrepreneurs aren't just making tech companies: they are making entertainment start-ups where their product is a technology experience.
- In some ways, a video game start-up is very much like a traditional start-up, but the pacing is much faster and the complexity of the work is tenfold.
- Independent developers are some of the riskiest kinds of entrepreneurs, because of the dynamic of the marketplace. So, it is imperative for them more than ever to prototype and iterate as much as possible.
- Indie developers live and die by their teams, whether it is one person or a handful of people — so choose wisely whom you rely on and be careful about how you divide and conquer.
- Tangible skills and perspective that will help one succeed:
  - How to manage time
  - Funding/Compensation (sustaining yourself)
  - How to mentor/teach others
  - How to work on a team/take on risk
  - How to always be consumer focused
  - Learn that failure is a good thing

ADDITIONAL INDUSTRY VETERAN PERSPECTIVE:

"It sounds like a terrible thing because it sounds like failure but you have to accept that failure is a crucial part of the creative process. Without accepting failure, embracing failure and always

hoping for failure, you are always going to struggle with creating something innovative."

— PETER MOLYNEUX (FOUNDER, LIONHEAD STUDIOS AND 22CANS)

"Thinking inside of the box and working with what you currently have, that is the challenge."

— JENNIFER BULLARD (DIRECTOR OF PROGRAM MANAGEMENT, QUERIUM CORPORATION)

"If you like video games, you can make your own job, create your own market and just befriend people, get friendly, get the word out there and it will go for you."

— DAVID VOYLES (SENIOR TECHNICAL EVANGELIST, MICROSOFT)

"It matters how you interact with your community and when you say something you got to hold yourself to it, when you do something right that's great, when you do something wrong you acknowledge it."

— FEARGUS URQUHART (FOUND AND CEO, OBSIDIAN ENTERTAINMENT)

CONCLUSION

SETTING THE WORLD ON FIRE

"It is not enough to learn, study, and practice. You at some point need to go up to the top of the mountain, and ski."

– CHRISTOPHER WEAVER (FOUNDER, BETHESDA SOFTWORKS)

You have now arrived at the concluding chapter of this book. All of the entrepreneurs and inventors you were introduced to have shared lessons with you—what to do, what not to do. But what about you? What is *the* most important lesson that you have learned in reading this book? While there are many important lessons revealed in this book, Christopher Weaver gives you his (and the right) answer in the quotation above. Entrepreneurship is action.

You can refine your idea many times before putting it into action, learn as much as you can about the keys to becoming a successful independent game developer, and hone your skills and talents in a classroom or controlled environment. But in order to succeed, you must act.

There is no "secret sauce" to create the next big video game like *Minecraft*. The entrepreneurs and innovators in each of these chapters spoke to the necessary things to know in order to find entrepreneurial success in the video game industry. They include developing your skills of imagination, listening, and persistence; and remembering who you are: an (aspiring) indie developer who is also an entrepreneur. You are capable of much more than creating "art" or an "experience" in a game. You are creating a sustainable life for yourself and others while accomplishing something truly profound—or what Steve Jobs referred to as "a dent in the universe."

Unleashing the Creative Force: Imagination, Collaboration, Persistence, and Experience

In an article published in *Vice*, Ryan Benno, an environment artist at Insomniac games said this, "The challenge of making a game is sometimes like trying to build a house blindfolded. You can plan out where the walls will be, what the rooms will be like, how to make it stable and functional, but until you are actually in the space you don't actually know." This is the same dilemma every hopeful entrepreneur faces, and it is what makes the difference between a "wantrapreneur" and an "entrepreneur."

It is important to keep in mind that instead of doing everything you can to make a masterpiece in one "at bat," like Jonathan Blow did with *Braid*, you must start somewhere. Jonathan Blow, is but one example of the handful of highly successful indie developers you were introduced to in this book. And all of the indie developers met their challenges in a similar fashion—they worked hard, real hard; they kept at it; and they viewed each "mistake" as taking them one step closer to success.

In the same article, Bruce Straley, Game Director for several critically acclaimed *Uncharted* games, as well as *The Last of Us at Naughty Dog*, stated:

> "It's not just an obsession—it's trying to transmit something from inside of us as creators and manifest it using a team of programmers, artists, musicians, all the different departments that make up video game development. That's a challenge."

Every video game developer, whether they be AAA or indie, faces the same challenges. How a AAA developer is able to solve a given problem might be different than an indie developer due to differences in resources, team size, and time. But you have learned in this book that both types of developers are able to overcome those challenges. But, as you have also learned, the more capable an indie developer is, the more likely they have some degree of meaningful industry experience before they became an indie developer—experience matters.

An indie developer is not inherently better or worse than a AAA developer because they chose to pursue a route of pure entrepreneurship. Both types of developers are necessary in order for the video game industry to be the thriving and ever expanding $100+ billion-dollar industry that it is today. For every *Call of Duty* and *Grand Theft Auto* from AAA developers, there is a *Braid* and a *Gone Home* from indie developers. It is an ever-changing industry where innovation is rewarded through sales. All this means that it is an exciting place to be—and it is only going to get better.

As technology has improved, so have the opportunities for indie developers to find their niche. As written in the *South China Morning Post*:

> "The Internet helped change that. Widespread adoption of broadband meant games could be more easily downloaded, rather than accessed from a physical disc bought from a store."

This means that the barriers to entry to the video game industry are lowered for indie developers because distribution and access is no longer controlled by a few corporations. Technology has democratized the video game industry by creating more opportunities for indie developers like you.

Whether it is making a game on the Unity game engine, a development platform for developers to make all kinds of games (especially mobile), creating an app, making use of virtual reality, or taking advantage of publishers such as Microsoft and Sony who are looking for ways to differentiate their consoles to consumers, the opportunities are plentiful. Sony's marketing support of *No Man's Sky*, a game made by a small team of indie developers at Hello Games, was an ambitious project that ultimately failed, but as major companies take on more risks like these, an indie developer might be lucky enough to create the "*No Man's Sky* 2.0"—an ambitious game that actually delivers on its promises and succeeds where others had failed.

ACHIEVING ENTREPRENEURIAL SUCCESS: CHALLENGES AND OPPORTUNITIES

Steve Jobs once said:

> "Innovation has nothing to do with how many R&D dollars you have. When Apple came up with the Mac, IBM was

spending at least 100 times more on R&D. It's not about the money. It's about the people you have, how you're led, and how much you get it."

That is true for you, too, as an indie developer and entrepreneur. It is about daring to dream big dreams and being persistent long after most others might give up.

There is a prevailing myth that you must be a programmer or an artist of some kind in order to be an entrepreneur in the indie gaming scene. The honest truth is that, at an indie studio, much like any other start-up, these enterprises need people of all different backgrounds: artists, writers, designers, business minded leaders, lawyers, human resource specialists, financiers, and more. Much like in the AAA-space, which needs diversity in roles in order for a company to succeed, an indie studio needs the same capabilities. The roles of marketing, in particular a fascination with, understanding of and love for the playing audience, will help lead the industry to access untapped potential with a wider, more diverse playing audience. Business savvy and leadership are also incredibly important, and might make or break the chances for success at an indie studio by enabling improved time management and offering best practice approaches to breakthrough innovation. But as a start-up, it becomes your decision as an entrepreneur to evaluate the merits and importance of these factors and find a way to maintain a competitive edge in indie gaming and the video game industry at large. As an entrepreneur, you are able to make those decisions because you did as Christopher Weaver advised you to do, you went out and skied. But remember that choosing to ski provides the opportunity for an exhilarating and successful ride down the slope, but also carries the risk of failure of falling down as you misjudged the slope.

As Matt Hansen said, and Feargus Urquhart, Peter Molyneux, and many others all agreed, industry experience is one of the key defining aspects of the most successful indie developers. Matt posited that this was the case because they understand both the AAA world and the indie gaming world. As an aspiring entrepreneur in indie gaming, it is my hope that you recognize that regardless of what path you take, you take advantage of the wisdom and expertise of industry veterans. Industry veterans understand what it is like to work in the video game industry the best because of their first-hand experiences.

As it is with any start-up, having a solid understanding of the industry you hope to enter is a given. In addition, for indie game developers, you need to understand these pressing challenges facing the video game industry: the problem of "crunch time" (how to hold steady in such high stress windows of time) that has plagued the video game industry and recognizing the value and importance of diversity in the industry. Diversity is not just a creativity imperative for the industry, it is also a social justice issue, particularly in terms of gender and racial biases. It is absolutely critical for independent developers to take a stand on these issues for creativity and social justice reasons. Your audience will reward you for taking this stand. It is indie gaming that has been a space that has enabled women, people of color, and other marginalized groups to find their voices and participate in the video game industry; this needs to continue and grow. Building a diverse team will not only aid the development process but also reveal new gaming frontiers.

In looking to the future, virtual reality is an emerging market for video games and indie game developers. Oculus VR, Valve, and Sony are all actively investing in and making as accessible as possible for would-be indie game developers (entrepreneurs). Moreover, education, both in the case of virtual reality and non-virtual reality, is another area of opportunity that will see major growth considering video games are slowly but surely now getting seen as tools that can enhance education inside the classroom. Whether it through outright "gamification," such as a scoring system or a healthy competition, or something more subtle such as placing an emphasis on engaging and interactive storytelling, video games have the potential to reshape a classroom dynamic.

Another future emerging trend is independent video games

that will be able to have a greater social impact. *That Dragon, Cancer* (2016), a game based on when Ryan (Designer) and Amy Green (Writer) lost their third child, Joel, to cancer, won the "Games for Impact" Award at The Game Awards 2016. When accepting the award, Ryan Green said:

> "Often in video games we get to choose how we're seen. Our avatars and our tweets and the work that we do are all meant to portray the story that we want to tell the world about why our lives matter. But sometimes the story is written onto us or it's told because of us or in spite of us, and it reveals our weaknesses, our failures, our hopes, and our fears."

Video games, especially independent video games, which take on the innovations of virtual reality, the opportunities of a classroom environment, and the experiences of the human condition, are what have the greatest ability to define the video game industry. Games such as *Call of Duty*, *Candy Crush Saga*, and other multi-million dollar franchises are wonderful and are enjoyable, but as the video game industry matures, the games (indie games) that take on these more difficult subject matters in meaningful ways through the use of cutting edge technologies in unique ways will ultimately win.

Independent developers exist in an ecosystem that is constantly changing, where newer, bigger, and better games are getting made by multi-million-dollar development studios and publishing companies. But within that ecosystem, smaller, more personable and engaging stories can be told by indie games. Innovators such as Peter Molyneux, Richard Garriott, and Gordon Walton are but a few of the many people who have pursued independent games development.

Indie gaming is about taking the virtual sandbox that is the video game industry and being bold in the pursuit of trying new things. That is why independent developers are indispensable to the video game industry. The video game industry, as it was democratized by people such as David Helgason (Co-Founder, Unity Technologies) as well as the iPhone and the App Store, is poised to bring about the rise of indie gaming. Indie gaming is relatively popular in the video game industry. Examples such as *Braid* (2008), *Minecraft* (2009), and *Inside* (2016) are but a few of the hundreds of independent games that gamers can play today.

Independent games are already successful such that they can allow individual developers to thrive, such as with Jonathan Blow and *Braid*. This might not be the case in every instance, as evidenced by Matt Hansen in his discussion of how Double Fine Productions rents out parts of their office spaces, as an incubator, to small independent developer teams who are struggling to survive even with their critically acclaimed games that they have made.

If independent developers are able to capitalize on the fact that they are entrepreneurs and transform how they are perceived in the video game industry, they could make independent games more successful than independent films are in Hollywood. *Inside*, with its Game of the Year award nomination at the Game Awards 2016 proves how independent games can rival the best of the AAA games, most notably the critically acclaimed AAA-game *Overwatch* by Blizzard Entertainment. Think about what would have happened if *Inside*, a game that was hailed by critics as a *masterpiece*, had won the award. Independent developers and indie games have legitimacy in the video game industry, but that would have put them over the top. It would force another re-evaluation in the video game industry as to what it means to make great, engaging, innovative, and fun games. Companies such as EA with EA Originals, Sony with their attempt at *No Man's Sky*, and other companies are slowly taking an interest in how to elevate indie gaming, so it is likely that in the next 15-20 years indie gaming will have an even greater and more meaningful presence in the video game industry.

The video game industry brings in more revenue than Books ($24 Billion), Music ($15 Billion), and Hollywood ($38 Billion) do combined every year. This means that the sandbox is huge and there is a tremendous opportunity for "wantrapreneurs" to become independent game developers—entrepreneurs and innovators in the video game space. AAA games are here to stay, and they are great in their own ways, but as independent developers step up their games, so too do AAA developers need to do the same as well.

Setting the World on Fire: Learning from the Past, Leading in the Future

Without question the video game industry is vibrant, ever changing and ever open to the next innovation that will launch its next chapter of growth. Remember this book began by framing the size, scale and relevance of this industry. To refresh, there are $100 + billion in worldwide sales. In the U.S. alone, there are over 155 million Americans that play video games, an average of two gamers per household and four out of five households own a video game device. It is stunning to think that as an industry, just over 40 years old, it still has such a bright future, with seemingly limitless potential to remain ever more relevant to today's world, with offerings to engage and entertain a diverse world of current and would be gamers. I hope this book has revealed insights and sets of action that would open up career potential and success for the up and coming generation. I hope that it inspires men, women, individuals of every color, culture or combination, young and old, all to see the potential to participate in and succeed in this industry. Only then will we realize its fullest and brightest potential.

With all of that in mind, and the fact that the vast majority of developers in the industry are white males, the time is now for people of all different backgrounds to try breaking into the video game industry. Gamers love Todd Howard (*Elder Scrolls* and *Fallout*), Sid Meier (*Civilization*), Will Wright (*The Sims*), and many more visionary video game developers. Can you name other developers who are not white males outside of Hideo Kojima (*The Metal Gear Solid Series*) and Amy Hennig (*The Uncharted Series*)?

That is why the demographics, the rapid advancements in technology, and the emphasis on this particular issue mean that a new generation of indie developers is poised to shape and define the video game industry.

The video game industry is a story of imagination, innovation, and creativity. It all started with Ralph Baer, for in the beginning of the video game industry, there was Magnavox, and now there are many. To quote Ralph Baer, "You learn as you go along. You get into a hole, you dig yourself out of the hole by learning things."

Ralph Baer is right, and it was his philosophy that ultimately brought upon the founding of the video game industry in 1972. A little over a half a century later, and Ralph Baer's experiences are relevant now more than ever. Ralph Baer as an inventor and entrepreneur was the first independent game developer.

He, much like any *wantrapreneur* or *entrepreneur* in indie gaming can do, started a **revolution**. A new revolution can be sparked by the power of just one really good idea and the collaboration with others to make that idea become a reality. Your challenge—think about what one idea you want to pursue and then go set the world on fire.

"I'm convinced that about half of what separates the successful entrepreneurs from the non-successful ones is pure perseverance."
— STEVE JOBS (CO-FOUNDER AND FORMER CEO, APPLE)

ACKNOWLEDGEMENTS

___

In creating this book, I had the unique opportunity to interview many different people within the video gaming industry. Each conversation taught me something, each conversation was a chance to further explore my passion and love for gaming, and each conversation brought me one step closer to making this book a reality. Here are the individuals that have been part of my journey:

Ralph Baer ("Father of Video Games," inventor – the Magnavox Odyssey, held over 200 patents)
Sonja Ängeslevä (Product Director, Unity Technologies and Mentor, GameFounders)
Dan Brady (Former CEO, Blue Castle Games)
Jennifer Bullard (Director of Product Management Querium Corporation)

Demetrius Comes (Former Executive Director of Engineering, WB Games – Turbine)

Mark Cooke (CEO, Shiny Shoe)

Brett Douville (Independent Developer)

Blake Edwards (Player Relations Specialist, Riot Games)

John Erskine (VP of Publishing, CIG's Director of Studio Services)

Richard Garriott (Pioneer of the MMO – Ultima, and Creative Director, Portalarium)

David Helgason (Co-Founder, Unity Technologies)

Nate Mitchell (VP of Product at OculusVR)

Peter Molyneux (Creator of Fable, Founder of both Lionhead Studios and 22 Cans founder)

Michael Turner (Entrepreneur and Founder, We The Players)

Feargus Urquhart (Founder and CEO, Obsidian Entertainment Founder)

Rich Vogel (President, Battlecry Studios)

David Voyles (Senior Technical Evangelist, Microsoft)

Gordon Walton (President, ArtCraft Entertainment, Inc.)

Paul Trowe (CEO, Replay Games Inc.)

Matt Hansen (COO, Double Fine Productions)

Christopher Weaver (Founder, Bethesda Softworks and Co-Founder, ZeniMax Media)

I would like to acknowledge, Eric Koester (Founder & Chief Instigator, Kingmaker Labs), who both inspired me to write this book and acted as a resource throughout the entire writing process. Additionally, thank you Jason Nellis who acted as both a mentor and a coach.

I would also like to recognize everyone else who is not mentioned in my acknowledgements section for all of their contributions to help me make this book a reality.

65886177R00115

Made in the USA
Lexington, KY
27 July 2017